MEET CAREW, GARVEY, MUNSON, AND BROCK

CAREW:

"I've never had publicity like this before, and truthfully, it's been great for me. But I don't want the other guys to get bugged by it. I want them to be a part of it, not separated from me or from what I'm doing. None of this is going to make me any different. I know I'll always look back to what I had as a kid and where I came from."

GARVEY:

"With each passing day it began to look more and more as if Cey was the third baseman. He wasn't about to be moved out. I was hardly playing at all, just pinch hitting occasionally and sometimes not getting in for two weeks because I didn't have a position. I was really starting to get down. But finally I just said to myself, if I'm ever going to get anywhere with this team, I've just got to do it when the opportunity comes—any opportunity."

MUNSON:

"I can't go through another year like this, no way. The Series is going to hit me in a couple of days. But I was happier when we won the playoffs, just because of all the stuff we've been through and being under the gun all the time. I'm tired now. I'm happy it's over."

BROCK:

"As a kid I wondered what life meant for me, what life had in store for me. When I looked at everything around me it wasn't a pretty picture. I saw people unemployed, depressed. At night sometimes I'd lay in bed and look up at the stars, saying to myself: 'There has to be *something* better for me. All right, how do I go about getting it?'"

At Bat

Carew · Garvey
Munson · Brock

by Bill Gutman

**tempo
books**

GROSSET & DUNLAP
A FILMWAYS COMPANY
Publishers · New York

To my sister and brother-in-law,
Sally and Fred Weinstein

Carew, Garvey, Munson, Brock
Revised edition
Copyright © 1976, 1978 by Bill Gutman
All rights reserved
ISBN: 0-448-14766-1
A Tempo Books Original
Tempo Books is registered in the U.S. Patent Office
Published simultaneously in Canada
Printed in the United States of America

ACKNOWLEDGMENTS

The author would like to thank the publicity departments of the New York Yankees, Los Angeles Dodgers, Minnesota Twins, and St. Louis Cardinals for furnishing background material helpful to the preparation of this book.

And a special thanks for Bing Devine, vice-president and general manager of the Cardinals, and Jerry Zimmerman, former player and coach of the Minnesota Twins, for sharing their views on Lou Brock and Rod Carew.

CONTENTS

At Bat
Carew ★ Garvey
Munson ★ Brock

★ ROD CAREW ★

★ In 1977 the baseball world at large discovered Rod Carew. The game's insiders—the players, managers, and coaches—had known about him long before. Just ask any pitcher in the American League. But it wasn't until 1977 that the mass media picked up on the Minnesota Twins' first baseman, the best pure hitter in the game.

The truth was they just couldn't ignore him any longer, even if they wanted to. For Rodney Cline Carew turned in one of the most remarkable seasons in the annals of the national pastime.

For most of the year, Rod flirted with the magical .400 mark, a batting feat last accomplished by Hall of Famer Ted Williams in 1941. This was nothing new for Carew. He had made .400 noises before and was the man considered most likely to crack the mark if anyone playing today could. When the season was half gone, at the 81st game, Carew was hitting .402 with 123 hits.

"I think I can hit .400 if I get hot," Rod said, at the time. "But I'm not going to come out and say, 'Yes, I'll hit .400.' "

Rod's midseason performance made him the top All-Star Game vote-getter in either league and marked the eleventh straight time in his career that he was on the squad for the midseason classic. Suddenly report-

ers, writers, TV crews—you name it—were flocking
to Minnesota to do features on the 31-year-old native
of Panama, who had been playing baseball at a superb
level since 1967.

"I've never had anything like this before, Rod
said. "I've even had to change my phone number at
home."

While admittedly enjoying his sudden turn in the
spotlight, Rod had always kept a cool head during the
years when other, often less-talented players, were
splashed all over the sports pages of the nation's tab-
loids.

"I always think about Henry Aaron," he said, "and
how it took him nearly 20 years to get recognition. If
he could take it, so can I."

Like Aaron, Carew keeps a low profile. His style on
the field is smooth and silky. He doesn't grab attention. He doesn't belt 40 home runs a year, or sulk
when things aren't going well, or pop off to the press
if he's unhappy about something. As Twins' coach
Jerry Zimmerman put it:

"Rod is the kind of guy who gets along great with
everybody but doesn't mix in with other guy's
business. He doesn't go around talking a whole lot,
but he's willing to help everybody. Yet he doesn't stir
things up."

During Rod's super season of '77, a couple of his
teammates, Larry Hisle and Lyman Bostock, declared
their intentions of becoming free agents at the end of
the year. Both were having outstanding seasons and
would bring a hearty price on the open market. Bostock, for one, said he'd never get his due in Minnesota
because Rod was the kingpin there.

Strange, during the years that Rod played in the
shadow of Harmon Killebrew and Tony Oliva, he
never complained. At any rate, there are those who

say that Rod, now earning about $200,000 a year, could perhaps double that on the the free agent mart.

"I knew the free agent situation was there," Rod said, when he signed a new three-year pact in 1976. "I didn't have to sign. Some of the free agents who got big money aren't in my caliber, but that's not really my business. You can only buy so much with money. I'd prefer to finish my career here."

Things and circumstances can change, of course, but as of now, Rod Carew is a happy, contented person. He enjoys living in Minnesota with his wife and family, and doesn't see the need to offer his services to the highest bidder. Surely no one would argue that after his 1977 season he could command a huge contract.

Obviously, Rod didn't hit .400. But he didn't miss by much, finishing at .388, the highest mark in baseball since Ted Williams had an identical mark in 1957. His 239 hits were the most garnered by a major leaguer since Bill Terry had 254 way back in 1930. To put it into simple language, if Rod had squeezed eight more hits into his 616 at bats he would have had his .400 season.

In addition, Rod showed his clutch ability by driving in 100 runs for the first time in his career. And he did it with just 14 homers, an unusual occurrence. He also scored 128 runs, the most in the majors, had 38 doubles, 16 triples, stole 23 bases, and struck out only 55 times.

But Rod's super season should not have been a surprise. He's been pointing toward it for a long time. In fact, his batting averages from 1973 through 1977 were .350, .364, .359, .331, and .388. That comes out to a .358 mark for five seasons, almost unheard of today.

Rod's .388 also gave him batting title number six,

putting him in pretty fast company. The only players in baseball history who have won more are Ty Cobb (12), Honus Wagner (8), Rogers Hornsby (7), and Stan Musial (7). Ted Williams also had six. All those players are in the Hall of Fame, and it's becoming pretty clear that Rod Carew will be there someday, as well.

As for a .400 season, well, that's what creates the most excitement. Bill Terry was the last National Leaguer to do it back in 1930. Then came Williams in the A.L. in '41.

Otherwise, the few other .400 hitters accomplished their feats in the early days of the game, from 1900 to the early 1920's, when the game was vastly different. But Rod Carew plays it like they did then, and as the best pure hitter in the game he can put the ball anywhere at any time.

At the plate, he has no weakness. He can handle any pitch and any pitcher. He can hit to all fields in any situation. And when he goes into an occasional slump, he usually breaks out of it by bunting more. He can bunt better than any player in the majors. In fact, one year he beat out 25 of 37 bunts for basehits.

But Rod Carew didn't put on a major league uniform and promptly begin slamming hits all over the place, pushing bunts to precise spots, and handling every kind of pitch with relative ease. True, Rod had a large measure of natural ability. He hit .292 as a rookie in 1967 and was named American League Rookie of the Year. That season and every one since, he has been named to the American League All-Star squad.

Yet from the time he joined the Twins, Rod has been one of the hardest working players around. He takes batting practice incessantly, more than anyone else. He is a perfectionist when practicing his bunting. And he works hard on the bases and in the field.

In 1976 he moved from second to first, and now plays there smoothly and effortlessly. He's also made himself into one of the game's best base runners. In 1969 he really drove everyone nuts. He set a record by stealing home seven times during the year. Since then, many pitchers will come to a set position instead of taking a full windup when Rod is on third.

One rap on Carew during his early years was that he was just a Punch and Judy hitter with little run-producing power. But Rod always claimed that wasn't his job—not when the team had the likes of Killebrew and Oliva hitting behind him. But when the face of the club changed, so did Rod. Up to 1975 his best RBI total was 62. But in '75 he drove in 80, the next year 90, and in 1977 hit the century mark. And he did this without sacrificing his batting average and often hitting in the number two spot in the order.

But baseball wasn't the only thing Rod Carew had to work on. Born and raised in Panama, he came to New York City as a teen-ager with a language problem and specializing in a sport that doesn't really go over big in the city. Thus when he came up, Rod was pretty much of a suspicious loner, very sensitive to kidding teammates, and shy with fans and reporters. He was often a solitary figure, taking batting practice alone and doing wind sprints and exercises after the rest of the team had ended workouts for the day.

It didn't help when the sports world at large learned that Carew, a black Panamanian, had married a white girl who also happened to be Jewish. This prompted the sickies to creep out of the woodwork, and Carew received a bevy of hate mail and disparaging remarks at the ball parks around the league. This could have easily gotten the best of him; that is, if Carew's character wasn't basically strong and on very solid ground. Now, in his early thirties and at the peak of his career, the slender Carew is very sure of himself and his life, his goals and aspirations, his place in the world.

But to fully understand Rod Carew and his development into baseball's best hitter, it's necessary to go back to the beginning. It's not hard to understand why Carew is always moving on the ball field. After all, he got his start in life that way—he was born on a train.

Rod's family lived in Gatun, in Panama's Canal Zone, and when Olga Carew felt she was ready to give birth on October 1, 1945, she had to move fast. There was no hospital in Gatun, so she boarded a train that would take her to the hospital at nearby Colon. But she never made it. Young Rod Carew arrived right on that train. Fortunately, there was a trained nurse in the same car as Olga Carew, and then a doctor was located in the other end of the train. The doctor's name was Rodney Cline, so a grateful Olga Carew named her infant son Rodney Cline Carew.

So it was back to Gatun, where Rod spent his early years. The Carews lived in a poor section of the town. Rod's father was a house painter and worked very hard to provide for his wife and children. Rod remembers being poor but happy in those early years.

"Mom and Dad always tried to provide for us, even though we didn't have much money," he says. "I was lucky in that I never wanted the so-called luxury toys that other kids had. I didn't care for owning things like bicycles. There was just one thing that made me happy from as far back as I can remember, and that was walking around all day with a bat and glove."

This meant playing ball whenever he could, whether it be a full game or just hitting flies with two or three of his friends. Young Rod walked from park to park looking for the action. Sometimes he just practiced hitting tennis balls when he could find someone to pitch. Other times there were no tennis balls, and they had to use big wads of paper taped into a ball.

Baseball was extremely popular in Panama, as it is in many Latin American countries, so the young boys knew how to play the game. There was an organized Little League there, and Rod joined up as soon as he was old enough. That was the first time he really played for a team.

The boys were also familiar with the major leagues in America, and had many of the same heroes as boys in New York, Chicago, and Los Angeles. All the papers carried scores of the big league teams and stories of the top players. Blacks and Latins were just beginning to appear in the majors when Rod was young, and before long he began to dream about playing there someday, too.

When Rod was sixteen there was a crisis in the Carew household. His parents were separating. Olga Carew decided to take Rod and his three sisters away from Gatun and to America. She had remained in touch with the nurse who helped deliver Rod on the train and was urged by her to come to New York City. So that's where the Carew family went in 1962.

"I remember the night we came into New York on the plane," Rod recalls. "I was awed looking down at the lights of the city. It was an impressive sight. But I soon found I didn't really like it in New York. I didn't enjoy the crowds. I liked to be by myself. I still do."

It wasn't easy for Rod to be deposited suddenly on the streets of New York. He had to learn things in a hurry. He knew that blacks sometimes had it rough, and since he spoke with a heavy Spanish accent, it was even harder for him to find new friends.

He went to George Washington High School in Manhattan, where he also kept pretty much to himself, though the few friends he had quickly tuned him in to the ways of the streets.

But school wasn't really his style. Before long he began realizing what so many black and Spanish youngsters find out, that there just weren't many opportunities open for him, especially if he had no real skills. Before long, his old dream returned, and he began walking the streets, as he had in Panama, bat and glove in hand, looking for some baseball action.

Unfortunately, baseball isn't a game that adapts to the pavements of the big cities, especially today, when there are fewer and fewer good places to play. There have certainly been some fine ballplayers from the cities, but they've generally had a tougher time making it than their country cousins. To make the point, George Washington didn't even have a baseball team, eliminating a primary outlet and developing ground. But Rod didn't quit. He kept on searching.

"I just kept scouting around until I finally found a sandlot team, the Cavaliers. They played most of their games in the Bronx, and their home field was a sandlot right next to Yankee Stadium. None of the players knew me, but they let me try out. I remember how surprised they were that I could hit a ball so far because I was pretty thin at the time."

But Rod's experience in Panama had paid off. Naturally, he quickly became a star of the Cavaliers, a team made up mostly of South and Central American players, who, like himself, had come to America from their homelands.

It was hard to imagine what happened next. Rod had come to this country in 1962, several months before his seventeenth birthday. In the spring of 1963, he had begun playing sandlot ball with the Cavaliers.

The father of one of his teammates was a man named Monroe Katz. Katz was what is known as a "bird dog." That means he checked out local talent for a major league scout, in this case Herb Stein of the Minnesota Twins. Stein had a lot of respect for Monroe Katz, and as soon as he heard about the young infielder from Panama who could hit like the blazes, he arranged a tryout.

The tryout took place in the summer of 1963, just about a year after Rod came to New York. And it took place in the legendary big ball park next to the sandlot, Yankee Stadium. The Twins were in town to play the Yanks, and Rod got the chance to work out with the big club. He didn't blow it. He showed he could handle himself adequately in the field, but the thing that impressed everyone most was his hitting. Standing relaxed and easy on the left side of the plate, Rod began stroking the ball to all fields. He swung at everything, good pitches and bad ones, and he was making contact, spraying the ball with good authority. The more he hit, the more players and coaches gathered around to watch. If Rod was nervous he didn't show it. He just kept hitting until someone told him to stop.

It didn't take the Twins' brass long to reach a decision. Before the club left town they offered Rod a contract, with a small bonus, and he jumped at the chance.

"My head was swimming," he said. "I couldn't believe this was happening to me. It seemed as if I had just come to the United States with nothing really going for me, and within a year I was in a major league organization. I was nervous, I guess scared, but I wanted to make good."

Rod was still young, and the team didn't want to rush him. For 1964, they sent him to Melbourne,

Florida, so he could play and learn in the Rookie League. There was a great deal of instruction, many drills, many practice sessions, and some ballgames (37 for Rod). But in those 37 games Carew showed his hitting was for real. Consistent from start to finish, he batted .325, with 40 hits in 123 at bats. Most of them were singles; there were just 5 doubles and 3 triples among them. But he drove home 21 runs and stole 14 bases. It was a good start, and for 1965, he was promoted to Orlando in the Florida State League.

The season at Orlando turned into a tension-ridden turning point for Carew. Not because of his play, which was improving. It was his relationship with his teammates that was causing the problem. For the first time Rod was thrown together with all the various types of men that make up a professional baseball team. They're all different, and they're not always proverbial nice guys. There are the kidders, the guys who fool around, and the jealous ones who begin to realize they're not going to make it and take it out on the others. Rod was still a relative newcomer to many American customs, and in a sense naive to the ways of many people. Before long, some of his teammates began getting to him.

A man named Bob Willis was the manager of the Orlando team in 1965. Willis had a tough exterior. He was short and stocky, and he looked as if he'd mixed it up a few times in his youth. But he wasn't all that tough on his players and gave them a pretty free rein, as long as they produced on the field. So, at first, Willis wasn't aware of what was happening.

"I was out on the field for practice one day in the middle of the year when I couldn't find Rod. I looked all over the place. Everyone was out there but Carew. Rod wasn't the type of guy to skip practice. In fact, he always practiced longer and harder than anyone, so I knew something must be wrong.

"Then my kid, who was our bat boy, comes running up to me all excited, shouting something about Rod being in the locker room packing his bags. 'He says he's going home!' my son shouted.

"Man, I almost panicked. The guy was hitting over three hundred, and I'd already been told that Mr. Griffith [Calvin Griffith, owner of the Twins] was expecting Rod to be his next superstar. So when I heard he was packing, I took off like I was shot out of a cannon. When I got to the locker room, there was Rod, cleaning out his locker. I didn't know what to say, so I just asked what he was doing, as if I didn't know.

"'I'm going home,' he says. 'I'm quittin' baseball. I've had it.'

"So I said to him, 'Look, if you *walk* out, they'll *throw* me out. The owner will shoot me if I let you go.'"

Then the two sat down to talk. The problem was Rod's relationship to his teammates. He was a very sensitive young man, and according to Bob Willis, was interpreting many of the remarks made by teammates as racial slurs. The fact remains that Rod was one of the first black ballplayers at Orlando, and if history is any barometer, there was undoubtedly some resentment and some outright prejudice on the part of a few players.

Rod was also hitting over .300 for the entire season and had as good a chance as anyone of being brought up to the Twins. So there was also some jealousy. Rod remembers some of them yelling, "Blooper ball!" whenever he got a hit that wasn't a solid line drive. So it was a tense situation, one that made Rod pretty much of a loner. But he came to his senses and finished out the season. There was too much to lose, and walking out certainly wouldn't solve any problems.

Carew's statistics were encouraging that year. He had a .303 batting average in 125 games, including 133 base hits. This time he had 20 doubles, 8 triples, 1 homer, and 52 RBIs. He also burned up the Florida State League base paths with 52 steals. So on the field, Rod Carew hadn't disappointed anyone. He might have been brought up right then and there, but the Twins had a pennant-winning team in 1965 and decided to leave him in the minors for additional seasoning. So in 1966 he went to play for the Wilson team in the Carolina League.

The manager at Wilson was Vern Morgan, and it wasn't long before he realized that the talented Carew needed some special handling.

"Rod was quite moody when he first came here," said Morgan. "Maybe part of it was that he had spent the whole winter in the Marine reserves. And maybe another part of it was the experience at Orlando. I think both those things made him homesick, and the homesickness made him moody."

Morgan talked to Carew whenever he could, trying to explain things to the youngster and encourage him to stay with it. There was still the fear within the Twins organization that Rod might just pack up and leave. But finally, after hours of talk, which sometimes bordered on pleading, Manager Morgan seemed to crack the Carew barrier.

"Vern made sense," Rod remembers. "He kept telling me over and over that if I didn't make it to the big leagues I had wasted a lot of time. I'd be nowhere, he told me. Then he reminded me that while I was a good hitter and improving all the time, I was still making mistakes and was unsure in the field. And a lousy fielder can't make it in the bigs. So that was a start. From that point on, Vern and I worked very hard, as often as we could."

Morgan and Carew would often stay late at practice, and the manager would just keep hitting grounders at the second baseman. He hit them every way, fast, slow, to the right, to the left, at him, bouncers, grasscutters, and a few other kinds that defy description. Slowly, painfully, Rod's fielding improved. They even worked on Rod's hitting. Morgan watched the natural Carew stroke carefully. And whenever he thought he saw a minor flaw, the two men discussed it, and then worked on it.

Yet, on occasion, Rod still became depressed, discouraged, and dejected, and he talked about going home. In Vern Morgan's words. "He was his own worst enemy," and when he brooded, his batting average often dipped. Then one day an incident occurred which Vern Morgan says he'll never forget, for it changed everything. He remembers:

"We were playing in Burlington, North Carolina, and Rod was in one of his down periods. He suddenly said he didn't want to play. He said his foot was hurting him, but we both knew what the real trouble was. That was just an excuse. Anyway, we had a pitcher going that day who really needed a win. I don't remember exactly why, but he wanted that victory. And when he heard that Rod wasn't going to play, he became frantic. He ran into the clubhouse looking for Rod, who was sitting there, moaning over his foot. So the pitcher ran into the trainer's room and came back with some bandages and salve. Then he started pleading with Rod.

" 'Let me fix it for you,' he said. 'I'll bandage it up so you can play.'

"Well, he kept this up until Rod was forced to take him seriously. When he realized the pitcher wasn't kidding, he was stunned. The whole thing really made a deep impression on him. He went out there that day, got four hits, and won the game for us. And it was the last time he pulled the homesick number. After that, he was here to stay. He never refused to play again, because for the first time he saw that he was really wanted."

So Carew finished the 1966 season on a high note. He played in 112 games and batted a respectable .292, not as high as in past years but still good enough for the parent club to take a long look at him in the spring of 1967.

The Twins had been American League champs in 1965, but lost a hard-fought World Series to the Dodgers, 4 games to 3. They were a solid club at most positions, led by slugger Harmon Killebrew, top-hitter Tony Oliva, shortstop Zoilo Versalles, and pitcher Jim "Mudcat" Grant. It wasn't an old team, and the experts figured they'd be on top for some time.

But in the next couple of years, several key players inexplicably lost their touch. Shortstop Versalles, the league's Most Valuable Player in 1965, stopped hitting completely and was traded. Pitcher Grant, a 20-game winner in the pennant year, never came close again. Sluggers Bob Allison and Don Mincher stopped producing consistently, while catcher Earl Battey, a steady performer, simply began getting old. So when Rod came around for the first time in 1967, the club was ripe for some new faces.

The second baseman during the 1965 Series was Frank Quilici, who later became the club's manager. Quilici never proved to be more than a good utility player, so when Rod began looking sharp during spring training in 1967, he was promptly installed at second, with Quilici moving to third. The second base job was his. He had made the big leagues in his first try. When the 1967 season opened, twenty-one-year-old Rod Carew was standing out at second base for the Minnesota Twins.

It was hard to figure what Rod's place in the game would be then. He came up without much advance notice, except for the Twins' officials who had high hopes for him. But the league at large wasn't expecting anything special. Just another spray hitter without much power was the general consensus.

It's necessary to look at a bit of baseball history to fully appreciate the prevailing attitude toward the likes of a Rod Carew in 1967. To do this, it's necessary to return to the beginning, to the turn of the century, when major league baseball was in its embryonic state.

The game was decidedly different then, much of the difference dictated by the times as much as anything else. Ball parks were smaller, of course, but they were also much rougher (there were no smooth infields). The dirt was rocky and rough and was hard to play on. Astroturf, or an artificial surface, wasn't even a pipe dream of the most imaginative of men.

Then there was the equipment, most notably the gloves, which were small and flat. The glove's purpose was just to protect the hands of the fielders. They were almost a hindrance instead of a help in picking up a ground ball. There were no deep self-sustaining pockets to make one-hand grabs and lunging stops automatic. Such plays came strictly through the merits of the individual fielders. So rule number one was that any ball—bouncer, grounder, or chopper—hit to the infield, had a good chance of somehow getting through.

The ball, of course, was made differently, and it simply didn't carry. It didn't leap off the bat and fly out to the far reaches of the ball park. In a sense, when hit, the ball just died. Hence, the era of the "dead ball." And although outfield fences were generally closer to the plate then, it still took a mighty wallop to hit one out. So the league's big "sluggers" might hit eight to ten homers a year, if they were lucky.

So where did that leave the good hitters? It left them with an attitude best exemplified by the legendary Wee Willie Keeler, one of the best of the turn-of-century batsman. Asked about his hitting philosophy, Keeler answered quickly:

"I hit 'em where they ain't."

Today, that's one of the most famous lines in baseball annals, a maxim that will live on as long as the national pastime is played. But when stated, it contained a barrelful of truths. The fine hitters of the day were truly bat manipulators who literally hit 'em where they ain't, deftly placing the ball between infielders, in the outfield gaps, down the lines, bunting when they caught the infielders deep, chopping it past them when the infielders were in close. They rode with the pitch, trying to make contact. Sometimes they intentionally swung down, blasting the ball right down onto the rough dirt of the infield. Whereas a two-base hit today is usually achieved on a hard outfield shot, doubles then were often the result of surprise tactical base running or of balls that died on long outfield grass or hit a rock and skipped past a fielder. Very few players uppercut the ball or had thoughts of hitting high long drives to the outfield. There was no percentage in doing that, not if one wanted a base hit.

As a consequence, there were plenty of outstanding hitters in the first two decades of the century, men who regularly hit in the upper .300s, with the .400 average almost a yearly occurrence by one or more players in either league. Shoeless Joe Jackson once batted .408 and didn't win the American League batting title. It sounds impossible, but it happened back in 1911, when a player named Ty Cobb batted .420.

Ty Cobb, the Georgia Peach, is widely considered the best hitter of all-time. In 24 big league seasons, from 1905 to 1928, Cobb had a lifetime batting average of .367, a totally incredible figure. He batted over .400 three times and took 9 consecutive batting championships, from 1907 through 1915. Then after a year off (hitting only .371), he took three more batting titles. Cobb won his last batting crown in 1919, yet after that he had years of .389, .401, .378, and .357 without taking the crown.

Anyway, Ty Cobb is considered the epitome of the early bat handlers who could get a base hit in so many ways. He was a left-handed batter who kept his hands spread several inches apart on the bat, allowing for better control. He could slide his lower hand up, or drop his top hand down, depending on where he wanted to place the ball. And he changed his stance to fit the situation and to throw the opposition off balance. Ty was also a master bunter and base stealer. That was his game. Anything to win.

Ty Cobb believed that hitters weren't born, that they learned the art through trial and error and through constant practice. He felt that his kind of hitting was a purer form of baseball than swinging for the fences. And in his autobiography, completed shortly before his death in 1961, he wrote:

"Boys, strive to master the lost arts of a great game. Unless you dedicate yourself to that task now, as the old timers die off one by one, they will have vanished forever."

Ty had plenty of reason to pen those words. For in the early 1920s, the game of baseball began to change. It changed principally because of one man and because of the crowds he was able to attract by swinging the bat in a big, new way. When George Herman "Babe" Ruth unexpectedly shattered all existing records with 59 home runs in 1921, people saw exciting new possibilities for the grand old game. Suddenly, a new ball was coming out, a livelier one that jumped off the bats as if it had been shot from a cannon. Ruth was truly an extraordinary slugger, as was teammate Lou Gehrig. But before long other sluggers were coming along, and the home run became an integral part of the game.

The long ball probably reached its zenith in the 1950s and early 1960s. It was the beginning of the big money era, and the big money was being paid to the big men who could drive the ball a country mile. More home runs were being hit than ever before, and more players were considering themselves sluggers. Most of the top players of that day were the men who could put the ball in orbit with one swing of the bat—Mantle, Mays, Aaron, Killebrew, Robinson, Matthews, McCovey, Colivito, Howard, Hodges, Snider, Campanella, Stargell, and on and on. True, many of them were fine all-around players, but the emphasis was truly on the home run.

Then, gradually, in the 1960s, things began to change again. Players who knew they couldn't hit 50 home runs a year began to concentrate on other things. In 1962, Maury Wills of the Dodgers shocked the baseball world by stealing 104 bases, thus reviving an art that had been dormant for decades. Suddenly, young players everywhere began stealing once more.

And about that same time a player named Pete Rose came up with the Cincinnati Reds and began banging base hits all over the lot. Rose wasn't just a little guy who got Punch-and-Judy hits. He was a stocky, powerful player who likened himself to a throwback of days gone by. Rose soon picked up the nickname of "Charlie Hustle, began attracting new fans, and then proclaimed:

"I'm going to be the first $100,000 singles hitter!"

Until then, the super big contracts were always reserved for the sluggers. Rose was the prime mover in changing all that.

So a new era began to dawn. Pirate outfielder Roberto Clemente was suddenly getting more recognition than ever before. He, too, disdained the home run for batting average, and people began to admit that he was every bit as much a superstar as sluggers Mantle, Mays, and Aaron. In the World Series of 1967 and again in 1968, one of the brightest stars was Cardinal outfielder Lou Brock, who had 25 base hits and 14 stolen bases in those two World Series and produced as much excitement as any slugger possibly could.

This brings us right back to the debut of Rod Carew. He had played his game the same way from the start. He knew he wasn't a slugger. Some others, including Brock, had to learn about themselves the hard way, but the new ball parks, with distant fences, taught the lesson quickly. And with Pete Rose earning the big money with his singles bat, others had hope and didn't try to alter their basic styles. Rod was one of them. As soon as he got to the big leagues, he went about working to perfect the things he did best.

It didn't all come together overnight, but Rod was still plenty good during his rookie year. He flirted with the .300 mark all season long, was voted the starting second baseman on the All-Star team at midseason, and finished with a .292 mark in 137 games (collecting 150 hits and surprising everyone with 8 homers and 51 RBIs). He won the American League's Rookie of the Year prize handily, and he seemed to be at the beginning of a fine career.

The next year a few doubters emerged, because

Rod had his poorest season at the plate. He had a bad knee part of the year, which limited him to 127 games. He also had the longest hitless streak of his career. He recalls:

"I was 0-for-17 and really starting to press. Then I hit a line drive and the outfielder almost made a spectacular catch but dropped it. I had 9-for-10 after that and I was on my way."

Though Rod made the All-Star team again in 1968, he had an offseason, hitting just .273. It was partly the bad knee and partly his unfamiliarity with the league and his need to work even harder. Perhaps his confidence was still not what it should be. But in 1969 he gave an indication of what was to come.

This was the year Carew took his first batting title, emerging from the pack to post a .332 average. Once again, minor injuries limited him to 123 games, but he still managed 152 hits in 458 at bats, including 30 doubles, 4 triples, 8 homers, and 56 RBIs. Being a free swinger he walked just 37 times, and he swiped 19 bases. But it was the steals that got him his first real bit of solid notice. For of those 19 steals, 7 of them were steals of home.

"I would have had even more, but during the entire second half of the season whenever I got on third, the pitchers came to a stop position instead of taking the full windup. Since pitchers don't like to do this with a man on third. I can only hope I helped throw their timing off somewhat."

Despite his first batting crown and first taste of notoriety, Carew wasn't a completely happy man in 1969. Occasionally he still became depressed and tended to brood, and he still harbored suspicions about some teammates, a few of whom had been on that Orlando team back in 1965. So he kept pretty much to himself and his reputation as a loner grew. But during that year, something happened that was to change Rod's life and actually put him to another kind of test. That was the year he met his future wife.

It seems like a simple enough thing on the surface; after all, Rod was at an age when many men get married. But there was a difference. Rod was at a night-club one night when a man, trying to impress his date, walked over and told the girl he wanted her to meet Rod Carew.

"Rod who!" was, in effect, what the girl said. Her name was Marilynn Levy. She was white and Jewish. Rod, being black and a Latin, would seem to be at the complete opposite pole. But the two of them hit it off immediately and were soon seeing each other regularly.

"Marilynn didn't know anything about baseball when I first met her," Rod recalls. "And when she was told that I was a pro ballplayer, what some people call a 'star,' the news didn't impress her one bit."

In a sense, dating Marilynn created a potful of potential problems for Rod. Interracial dating and marriage was still frowned upon with varying degrees of belligerence, and he knew exactly what to expect. Yet he played better than ever on the field, taking his first batting crown, and in the offseason, his relationship with Marilynn became even more involved. Finally, they became engaged.

"At first, Marilynn's parents were very negative about us," Rod says. "Her mother didn't even want to meet me until one day when we were both invited to dinner at Marilynn's sister's house. It was the night we got engaged, and as it turned out, Marilynn's mother and I were both in for a surprise. We hit it off real well. The only thing she asked me that night was, 'Please, take care of my little girl.' "

Rod and Marilynn were married in early 1970, and Rod says he never personally thinks about their union in terms of black and white.

"I love my wife," he has said. "We enjoy each other's company; we understand each other. I never think of my wife as being white. I just think of her as being a woman."

Unfortunately, there were people who didn't see it that way, and Carew admits that he's received his share of obscene letters, especially a few years after the marriage when it was learned that he was studying the Jewish religion.

"There are a lot of sick people in the world," Carew said. "I always knew people would say there are two strikes against me. I'm a black man who is going to be a Jew. I've gotten a lot of bad mail, but it just boils down to what a guy wants to do with his life. People are not going to scare me away from it.

"But the mail started as soon as we were married. There were things like, 'You're gonna be shot at as you walk out of the plane.' There were a couple of threats like that. Then it was mostly black-white. Now there are things like, 'Hitler had the right idea, he ought to do the same thing to blacks that he did to the Jews.'

"Yet I'm not really surprised. Blacks went through the same thing. Only I didn't realize it was the same for others until I read how bad it's been for Jews. But Marilynn's attitude toward it has always been the same as mine. I remember an uncle of hers asking if she was marrying me because I was a star and on top. She said no, she wasn't marrying me because I'm a ballplayer, but for better or worse."

So the Carews have become a close family despite the adversity, and they treasure their moments alone, enjoying each other and their two children. Rod's marriage surely made him a stronger, more mature, and happier person. His old manager, Vern Morgan, is one who noted the change:

"Rod's like a lot of people in any kind of profession. He's grown up since the year I had him at Wilson. He's become a man."

Carew also continued to grow on the ballfield. In 1970 he was off to his best start ever, batting up around the .370 mark when his season came to an abrupt end. The Twins were playing the Milwaukee Brewers. Mike Hegan was on first and took off to second on a grounder. Carew cut over to take the throw from short, then pivoted and fired to first. A second after he released the ball, Hegan barreled into him, leaving the second baseman writhing in pain. Ligaments in his right knee were torn, requiring immediate surgery. He didn't get back until the final few weeks of the year.

The incident upset Rod, who has always been known for his gentlemanly play. He intimated that Hegan could have stopped:

"The play was over; I had already thrown the ball. But he just kept coming."

Carew admitted that the collision caused him to be gun-shy at second for a couple of years, until he was entirely convinced that the knee was back to full strength. He had watched teammate Tony Oliva's career ruined by bad knees, and he didn't want it to happen to him.

The incident also confirmed Rod's way of playing the game. Though he had been hurt, he still never tried to hurt anyone else, a statement many of baseball's so-called tough competitors can't or won't make.

"I avoid hurting someone whenever possible," Carew said. "Reggie Jackson came into second once in 1974 and stood up on a double play ball instead of sliding. It would have been easy to hit him with the ball. But I knew he had a bad leg, a hamstring pull, and probably didn't want to risk sliding. So I went well out of my way to throw around him, and later he thanked me for it."

A player doesn't have to be a brawler to be a winner. In the 51 games he played in 1970, Carew hit .366. Had he not been injured, he undoubtedly would have had an outstanding year and most likely would have taken another batting title. In 1971 he stayed healthy, although he favored the knee somewhat, hitting .307 in 147 games. Then in 1972 he started his string of batting titles with a .318 mark. Finally, in 1973, he had his first super year, batting .350 and getting some of the recognition he deserved.

Part of his recognition came slowly because of the Twins. The team had gone downhill since 1965, and it was now trying to rebuild. Carew was its one shining light, but it's not easy getting publicity playing with a mediocre team in Minnesota.

Yet more people within the game began to recognize Carew's talents, ask him about his hitting, and study his techniques.

"My own theory is to swing the bat," Carew said. "If the ball's around the plate, swing and make contact. It's kind of a Latin tradition. I grew up that way in Panama. Here a lot of guys look for certain pitches in certain areas. But you may never get those pitches. I hate to take a pitch. If I could be a guess hitter I'd hit 500! But I don't like to think too much about hitting. I like being up there, not guessing, just getting up there and swinging free."

Some of Rod's opponents feel that kind of statement is a put on. As pitcher Ken Holtzman says, "He has an uncanny ability to move the ball around as if the bat were some kind of magic wand."

And Frank Robinson said, "Rod swings the bat about as perfectly as anyone I've seen."

Perhaps one writer summed it up best when he said, "Although Carew persists in his claim that he is a free swinger who doesn't plot out his hits, the suspicion is growing around the league that if arbitrators demanded doubles that rolled dead exactly 385 feet from the plate, or ground balls whose big hops measured exactly 11 feet at the crest, or line drives over the pitcher's left shoulder, Carew would contrive to turn out those, too."

In other words, there are a growing legion of fans who feel that Rod Carew can do just about anything he wants with a bat. Yet Rod still insists he's not all that accurate.

"Hitting is an art, but not an exact science," he says. "Outfielders tend to play me like a right-handed hitter. That leaves me a hole in right field. If I could do it, I'd get a hit every time by just going for that hole. But I can't do it. Usually when I try to pull the ball I hit off my front foot and can't get anything behind on my swing. So I just concentrate on hitting up the middle or going to the opposite field."

Maybe hitting isn't an exact science, but Rod Carew has worked to make his hitting as perfect as possible. The great Ted Williams once said that hitting a baseball was the single most difficult task in all of sports. During the tenure of his lengthy career, Williams hit every chance he had, often begging pitchers and coaches to stay late and throw him more batting practice pitches. Williams said that many of today's players don't do that. They just take the prescribed number of swings in the cage and get out. And as a consequence, their hitting never improves. And using the Williams theory, Rod Carew is a hitter after his own heart.

"I'm different than a lot of young hitters I see today," said Carew, in 1975. "We had a day off Monday, and I took ten extra minutes of batting practice on Tuesday. I take all the extra BP I can get. Guys who are hitting .190 and .220 should be doing that, and they don't. They should be asking questions, and they don't. It's a funny thing about some ballplayers. They get to the big leagues and they stop trying to learn; they don't think they have to try to improve. I've tried to tell some guys the things they're doing wrong. But they just keep doing them over and over again."

There was a time when Carew had trouble with high, inside fastballs. So he worked at it and finally learned how to handle that pitch. He's done the same with any other weakness he felt he had.

"You have to work and discipline yourself," he says. "A guy has to know what kind of hitter he is and has to know his limits. I've seen guys who make an out and come back and break their bats and helmets. Hell, the pitchers are getting paid to get you out, too. I always had the attitude that if a guy gets me today, I'll get him tomorrow."

Another weapon in the Carew arsenal is the bunt. Rod has gotten up to 29 bunt hits a year. He also has used the bunt to get himself out of slumps, much the same way Ty Cobb once did. Understandably, Rod is quite proud of his bunting and the work that goes into keeping that lost art finely tuned.

"Even when they know I'm going to bunt they can't throw me out," he says, forgetting modesty for the first time. "I can drop the ball to a spot where they will have an awkward throw. They have to come up clean with the ball and throw on the run. Not too many third basemen can do that consistently."

In the spring, Rod will practice his bunting upwards of 45 minutes a day, and he'll always take 15 minutes of bunting before every single game. It's the start of his pregame batting practice, which is carefully calculated and shows him to be the true hitting artist he is.

"All some of these guys want to do in batting practice is put the ball in the seats," Rod says. "I concentrate on moving it around."

So he begins, dropping bunts to different spots along the third and first base lines, then between the mound and the lines at varying distances from home plate. After about 15 minutes he starts to swing away—with a purpose.

At first he'll just bounce balls right up the middle of the diamond into centerfield. Then when he's satisfied, he'll adjust his swing and begin cracking solid line drives down both lines, left and right, picking his spots and putting the ball there. Finally, he'll hit some into the outfield gaps and then take one or two roundhouse swings for kicks. As one writer put it:

"For all his modesty about placing the ball, he is as accurate as an archer."

In 1974, Rod made his first run at .400, or at least got a lot of people thinking about it as he flirted with the magic mark right through the end of June. A look at the batting races in both leagues showed something very interesting. Seven of the top ten hitters in the National League and six of ten in the American could be considered Carew-Rose singles-type men. There seemed to be a revival of an old baseball tradition and ancient baseball art—bat maniuplation.

Carew himself used a light, 32-ounce bat for maximum handling. This way, he could easily adjust to changing game conditions. There was a late-June game against the Orioles in which Carew was 0 for 4 at bats entering the ninth inning. The horsecollar had dipped his average below .400; besides, he hates so-called "oh-four" games. Since so many of Rod's hits got up the middle, Oriole shortstop Mark Belanger and second sacker Bobby Grich were both cheating, playing close together near the bag. Grich had already taken away a couple of potential hits, one of which would have brought home the tying run a day earlier.

This time Rod wasn't about to get nailed. He waited a split second longer on a pitch and drilled it through the hole at shortstop where Belanger should have been playing. The next night Grich and Belanger moved back to their natural positions, and Carew promptly slammed two hits right up the middle. His average was back to .399 and talk of a .400 season continued.

"If Rod gets lucky and stays healthy, I think he can hit .400," said his then-manager and former teammate, Frank Quilici. "He has so many offensive gifts. He has great speed and beats out a lot of ground balls. In fact, as far as I'm concerned, there's nobody alive—nobody—who can turn a single into a double and a double into a triple the way Rod can. And when he isn't hitting he can always bunt for hits. Now, after seven years in the league he's really found himself. He's around .400 now, and his hottest months are usually August and September."

Carew didn't really want to talk about .400 at this point. He wasn't ready to put more pressure on himself. "When you get goals you add pressure," he said, "and there's enough of that already. You know, I'm pretty much of a free swinger, and I don't walk too much. I think I walked 62 times in 1973, while Ted Williams had something like 145 walks when he hit .406 in '41. And now, with so many good relief pitchers around, you're always facing somebody fresh. Every team has three or four good starters and a couple of very good relievers. That's a lot of pitching."

In 1974 the National League's answer to Rod Carew was Ralph Garr, a speedy, freeswinger with the Atlanta Braves. He was hitting about .370 in July of that year, and was also being mentioned as a possible .400 candidate.

"Nothing is impossible," said Garr, "but for someone like me and Rod to hit .400, we'd have to get about 250 hits. Tough but not impossible. I probably try to hit the ball harder than Carew, so I top the ball a lot, but I beat out a lot of those rollers. I usually just hit the ball where they pitch it to me, but I won't always try to go to left on an inside pitch. And in certain situations I might go for the home run. I take whatever comes."

Carew saw it more as a matter of his job:

"Certain guys on certain clubs have a job to do. My job is to get on base, to try and hit the ball somewhere. On this club we always had guys to drive in runs. But they've got to have somebody on base to do it. Every hitter knows his capabilities. I know mine. I could hit the ball hard if I wanted to. But if I hit 10 home runs I'm not going to help this club. If I get on base and score 95 runs, I am."

Manager Quilici agreed. "Rod could be a different type of hitter if he wanted to. He could hit maybe 20 or 25 home runs. I've seen him hit the long ball. I remember one long blast in the old Kansas City ball park that cleared the equipment house in centerfield, well over 400 feet away. But he never thinks home run. He thinks line drive."

But a .400 season is no easy feat. By late July and August it seemed out of reach, and when the season ended, Carew was "down" to .364, still a better average than most players today ever hope to reach. He also had 218 hits in 599 at bats, 30 doubles, 5 triples, 3 homers, 55 RBIs, and 38 steals. It was certainly a super season, his second in a row, and it was his third successive batting crown.

Carew was a much more secure man than he had been in earlier years. Though not a holler guy, he now considered himself a team leader, who did his thing by example rather than words. It was a far cry from his early days when he took objection to a teammate's remark and the two went into a broom closet to have it out. So many teammates piled in to watch that there just wasn't room for a fight. Finally, everyone just broke up in laughter.

He had the same kind of control and security on the field, as former Detroit Tiger catcher Bill Freehan observed.

"Rod has control of his whole game," said the veteran. "He never lets it get away."

With two super seasons behind him, Rod felt he was in line for a big raise. He asked for $140,000, but owner Calvin Griffith offered just $120,000. When neither party would budge, the dispute went to arbitration, where a judge ruled in favor of Griffith. Carew was angered and determined to make up for it with another super season. He was also annoyed by some remarks attributed to Griffith, describing him as an error-prone second baseman and a singles hitter. There was still that old prejudice in favor of the power men.

"I thought I was a member of the Twins' family," Rod said, "but I guess I'm just a number instead. We'll see what happens this year."

Before the 1975 season started, someone decided to compare Carew's .323 lifetime average with that of the late Roberto Clemente after Clemente had played nine years. Clemente, who wound up at .317, did considerably better after thirty years of age. He was just at .303 after nine years. And if that happens with Carew, watch out!

Thus 1975 began, and for the first month and a half or so, Carew was struggling, at least for him. He was hitting *only* .346 and not even leading the league. Then suddenly, Rod Carew got hot, the kind of hot that defies description and boggles the mind.

He began to hit and hit and hit. Hits came in bunches, real bunches, like, say, five straight three-hit games. The whole thing crested in a three-game series against the Yankees when Carew had 12 hits in 13 times at bat. And in one of the games, against newly acquired Yankee ace Catfish Hunter, he blasted two opposite-field home runs, added another single, and drove in all four of his club's runs. And the 12 of 13 was extended to 26 for 42 when taken back a few more games. And that's a .619 clip. Take it back a few additional games and Carew was 35 for his last 59 trips, a .593 average. It was one of the hottest streaks ever and raised his overall season's average to .425. Once again the .400 talk started, but Rod was more interested in talking about his streak:

"The last ten days I've felt so confident that I think there's not a pitcher around who can get me out. I really don't think anyone can hit better than me."

Catfish Hunter, victim of the two homers, wasn't about to argue.

"He [Carew] has the quickest wrists I ever saw. There's just no way to pitch him, no way."

Another Yankee hurler at the time, Doc Medich, put it differently. "You just have to hope he makes a mistake," said Medich. "I know that sounds like the shoe being on the other foot, since it's usually the hitter who waits for the pitcher to make a mistake. But Carew's that good."

Writers and reporters again picked up the .400 theme, assembling statements from former .400 hitters. One had remarks made by Ty Cobb back in 1960 which seemed prophetic.

"Somebody will hit .400 again," Cobb had said. "Somebody will get smart and swing naturally."

Bill Terry, another .400 man, had this to say: "To hit .400 you need a great start and you can't have a slump. The year I did it, I was around .410, .412 all season, and I was really hitting the ball on the nose. Hitting is a business. With two strikes, you really protect that plate."

Then there was Ted Williams, who thought it would take something else. "To hit .400," said Ted, "you've got to have power to keep the defense back and spread out. And you've got to be fast."

Well, Carew seemed to have all the ingredients mentioned by the three greats except perhaps power. Yet Oakland centerfielder Bill North, a man who should know, disagreed.

"There's no way you can play him," said North, "because he can hit with enough power to keep you back deep so you can't play him like he's going to drop everything right over the infield. And he can drop it over the infield. Rod Carew is in a class by himself."

Others around the league agreed, saying that Carew had the best bat control of anybody in baseball.

"He just watches the defense and hits according to how they play him," said outfielder Jim Northrup.

And Bobby Grich, now with the California Angels, said, "With a man on first and the first baseman holding, I've seen Rod intentionally try to pull that ball through the hole."

Oriole hurler Jim Palmer claimed Carew "seems to

hit the ball where he wants to, which is something not too many can do."

Carew himself admitted that his favorite kind of hit is "just one inch or two outside a guy's reach. Maybe he cheated over a step in the other direction on me, and I kept him honest."

As for hitting .400, Carew always tried to choose his words carefully.

"It's much too early to say now," he quipped. "But if I'm hitting .385 at the end of August or in early September, then I think I might be able to do it. Last year it got to a point where I thought I might do it, so now I'm trying not to think about it."

That wasn't easy, especially when everyone else connected with the game talked of little else. But, following the pattern of the previous season, Rod gradually dropped off in July and early August, putting a .400 run off for at least another season. Yet he once again produced a year that few will ever match.

Limited to 143 games by some muscle pulls and minor injuries (something that always seems to plague him and could be a factor in a .400 bid), he won still another batting title (his fifth, fourth in a row) with a .359 average, collecting 192 hits in 535 at bats. But the real difference in 1975 was his power. With some of the Twins sluggers from past years gone or disabled, Carew upped his totals to 14 homers and 80 RBIs, the latter figure leading the team.

Despite Rod's personal success, the failure of the Twins to win a pennant really bothered him. In 1967, his rookie year, the team had a one-game lead with two left, but blew both games to the Red Sox, who won it. Then in 1969 and '70, they won the Western Division crown, but were beaten in the playoffs each time by Baltimore.

"I remember when we clinched the division in '69,"

Rod said, "a lot of the guys were celebrating with champagne. I kept telling them we hadn't done anything yet. And we hadn't. Not being in a World Series leaves me unfulfilled as a ballplayer. You work for that all season, every season. And no matter what else I do, I know I won't be satisfied until I play in a World Series and win it."

Not being on a championship team has been a bane for more than one great athlete. Basketball's Pete Maravich and football's O. J. Simpson are just two examples.

In 1976 he signed a new three-year contract with the Twins, ending rumors that he would become a free agent. Then he went about playing ball again. To some Carew watchers, 1976 was an off year. Rod started slowly and for most of the season was hitting *only* around the .315 and .320 mark. It didn't seem as though he had a shot at a fifth straight batting title.

Then in the final weeks of the season, with the Twins again out of it, he began surging. He kept climbing, and even came through with two hits in his final two plate appearances to finish at .331. The only problem was that a couple of Kansas City Royals, George Brett and Hal McRae, edged him out with .333 and .332 marks respectively.

For Rod, it was not a super year. Yet he received one first place vote in the league's MVP balloting, the first time in his career anyone had voted for him. But he was sixth in the overall standings behind winner Thurman Munson of the Yanks, the same Munson who, while catching against the Twins earlier in the year, said to Rod:

"Do me a favor. Watch me when I'm hitting and tell me what I'm doing wrong."

That's the kind of respect Rod has around the league. In fact, when spring training for 1977 rolled around, an interesting thing happened. The Twins were heading from Orlando to Tampa, Florida, to play the World Champion Cincinnati Reds. It had been announced beforehand that Rod would stay behind and miss the game. That's when he got a call from Reds' Manager Sparky Anderson.

"Rod, I'd really appreciate it if you could come over and give some of my players a bunting clinic," Anderson asked.

Rod agreed, and that afternoon conducted the clinic, tutoring the likes of Joe Morgan, the 1975 and '76 National League MVP, Ken Griffey, an all-star outfielder, and George Foster, the 1977 National League MVP. That's how much people in the game admired Rods skills. It was only much of the general public who was still in the dark.

As the 1977 season got underway, it was business as usual on one Minnesota front, but something entirely unexpected happened on another. The usual was that Rod was up among the league's leading hitters, well above the .300 mark. The unexpected was that the Twins were winning and battling for the division lead.

Besides Rod, the club was getting bat action from Hisle and Bostock, Glenn Adams, Butch Wynegar, Dan Ford, and Roy Smalley. The platoon players were also coming through, so the team was scoring a bunch of runs. They were also getting adequate pitching from starters Dave Goltz, Paul Thormodsgard, and Geoff Zahn, as well as outstanding relief hurling from Tom Johnson. The Twins had an exciting club for the first time in years.

Then in June, Rod got hot. Everyone knew by then what happens when Rod Carew goes on one of his streaks: he begins hitting at an incredible pace. And he can keep it up for weeks, smacking base hits off every kind of pitch, game after game.

The average began climbing: .350 . . . .360 . . . .370 . . . .380 . . . .390 . . . and finally over 400 once again He was back in his customary position atop all major league batters, and slowly but surely, the murmurs began. By July 1, Rod was up to .411 and the hoopla really started.

"During that hot streak Rod was just hounded constantly," recalls Twins' Coach Jerry Zimmerman. "*Time* Magazine had him; *Sport* Magazine was after him; he was doing things before the game with some of these people. They were going around town getting different pictures and things like that. I'm sure it had to work on his mind a little bit, but no one around him seemed to notice it.

"He handled himself very well. He was always willing to cooperate with people, as long as they treated him with respect. For instance, he won't sign an autograph for some fan if they'll yell things like 'Hey, Carew, sign it.' That kind of turns him off and I can't say that I blame him. You know, he's asked so often—and I've seen him sign so often—and then one person is so rude . . . I don't blame him."

Then Coach Zimmerman went on to talk about the kind of hitter that Rod Carew has been the past several years.

"He's capable of getting 15 straight hits," said Zimmerman, "but he's not capable of going 0 for 15. It might happen, but maybe three times in his career. Chances of him going nine for 15 are better than him going 0 for 15.

"He just doesn't have any particular weakness at the plate. They pitch him inside and he hits it to left field. There's just no way of figuring him out. I've seen him hit all types of pitches. There are some who give him a little more trouble, but they're the guys he's hitting .333 against. And he's hitting .500 or .600 against the patsies."

Like most great hitters, Rod is always observing, studying, looking for something that will give him an edge.

"Rod is always mentally prepared," Zimmerman continued. "He's always in the ballgame. Even in the dugout he'll bring something up to a guy about how a guy's pitching or his move to first base, little things like that. Little things that might help somebody.

"He knows he can hit, and he feels you don't have to make any outs. So he doesn't waste any times at bat like a lot of guys do. I mean he doesn't swing at bad balls, doesn't get anxious with men in scoring position. He's always the same hitter. He knows that every time at bat is a chance to get a base hit, where another player won't look at it that way. That's another reason he's such a great hitter, because he's constantly thinking, 'Now is my time to do something.' "

Both Rod and the Twins continued to ride high. Minnesota was battling for the A.L. West lead with Chicago, Kansas City, and Texas, and through most of the year it was the Twins or White Sox who led it, though the experts still felt the Royals would win.

Whenever Rod had threatened .400 in the past, he usually dipped below shortly before or after the All-Star break, and the excitement died down. This time he stayed up there. Perhaps the press and recognition came because we seem to be in something of a record-breaking era. First there was Hank Aaron, topping Babe Ruth's home-run total, then Lou Brock setting single-season and career-stolen base records. Marks that had stood for up to half a century were being beaten by the modern players. So it's understandable that most fans were pulling for Rod to make it.

"I've never had publicity like this before," Rod said, "and, truthfully, it's been great for me. But I don't want the other guys to get bugged by it. I want them to be a part of it, not separated from me or from what I'm doing. None of this is going to make me any different. I know I'll always look back to what I had as a kid and where I came from."

Then in August two things happened almost simultaneously. Rod's pace began to slow, and the Kansas City Royals began winning big. Rod didn't really slump, but instead of getting three hits, he'd get two, or instead of two, one. There was no sudden drop, but slowly, the average dipped below .400, then below .390, then below .380. It began to look as if he wasn't going to make it after all.

But interestingly enough, where in the past people forgot about Rod as soon as the average went under .400, this time they didn't. The lesson seemed to sink in. The man was baseball's best hitter, and no one could argue about it any longer. Never again would he be Rod who? From where? And with what team?

By August 30, the Twins lead had been cut to two games. The Royals were hot and breathing down their necks. And Rod's average was down to .377. There were 28 games left in the season and some people figured Rod might be down to .350 before it ended.

In those last games the Twins continued to falter as the Royals became the hottest team in baseball. K.C. bolted into first place and proceeded to make what had been a hot race a runaway. With chances of a World Series gone down the drain and .400 looking like a pipe dream, no one would have blamed Rod for letting up during those last few weeks of the year.

But he didn't. Instead he dug in and played the best

ball he possibly could. Over the final 28 games of the year he hit .441, banging the ball all over the lot. But when you're hitting in the upper atmosphere and with so many at bats, the average comes up ever so slowly. Despite the rousing finish, Rod's average went up just eleven points to give him his final .388 log.

Yet, in reality, he hadn't missed by much. By the margin of eight hits, to be exact. As one observer pointed out, if Rod had been playing in the National League with all those fast artificial surfaces, he surely would have had the eight hits.

That, of course, is hard to say. There are certainly many plus and minus factors. For instance, Rod batted .418 by day and .367 at night. So if there wasn't night baseball like in the old days. . . .

But facts are facts. Rod closed strongly despite the fact that the Twins lost 19 of their final 28 games and finished 17½ games back, which makes his performance even more remarkable. He kept his concentration in spite of everything. Jerry Zimmerman looked at it this way:

"The pennant race might have spurred him mentally because I know he'd like to be on a winner," said the coach. "But he's just the kind of guy who's gonna do his best at all times. He's a special kind of guy who never quits."

Maybe Rod didn't hit .400, but his .388 mark and sixth batting title, as well as his .334 (and climbing) lifetime average, are rapidly putting him up there with the game's elite. And after the season ended the accolades continued to come in.

First he was named to the major league All-Star team once more. Then he won a special award, sponsored by a beverage company, which named him as "the most consistent and most productive" player in baseball. That gave him a $10,000 prize and the knowledge that he had beaten out Cincinnati slugger George Foster, who was the National League's Most Valuable Player on the strength of a 52 home-run, 149 RBI season.

And shortly afterward everything was topped off by Rod's being named the Most Valuable Player in the American League for the first time.

"This is great," Rod said. "I'm happy the way I won it because there was a lot of competition. I wasn't sure I'd get it if the team didn't win, but obviously the things I did were taken into consideration and I'm very happy it came out this way."

So where to now? Rod is certainly at his peak, but the years are beginning to mount. Can he still have a .400 season? Most of those around him feel he can do it if all the conditions are right. Rod himself is a bit more skeptical.

For one thing, the Twins lost their other two best hitters, Larry Hisle and Lyman Bostock, to the free agent mart. So just when it looked as if the team was building, it suffered a setback.

"I don't like the idea of carrying the load on my shoulders all the time," Rod said. "It gets to be too much. I'll always try my best, but I can't do it all by myself."

So that's an added pressure on Rod. In addition, he pointed to the fact that he was tired at the end of 1977, despite his strong finish.

"Yes, I was very tired at the end of the year, and it gets harder every season."

You wouldn't know that by the stats. To many, it seems that Rod Carew gets better every season. He keeps himself in fine condition and is by no means too old for another few assaults on the magic mark. After all, there have been other fine players who have improved with age.

But no matter if Rod has that .400 year or not, he's certainly going to leave his mark on the game of baseball. His lifetime average is already up there with the greats. He's just 103 hits short of 2,000, so he's got a shot at eventually joining the select 3,000-hit club.

And perhaps most of all, he's shown fans and players of the modern era that the art of hitting a baseball is not gone. It's been reborn, in the person of Rod Carew.

★ STEVE GARVEY ★

★ In a sense, it's all too perfect. But then again, it's all true, and you can't change that. If they decide to make a movie out of it, the title is a natural: *Born to Be a Dodger*. The subtitle? *The Steve Garvey Story*.

It's the way stories used to be: young boy becomes team bat boy; idolizes popular, clean-cut first baseman; pursues own career; winds up playing first base for the same team; becomes star and Most Valuable Player, then tells reporters:

"I sincerely think I was born to be a Dodger."

Fade out. The perfect ending—unless you want to show the hero jogging into the sunset, glove and bat in hand, with the doors to the Hall of Fame opening wide to greet him. That part of the story hasn't been played out yet, but the way Steve Garvey has been going, can it end any other way?

Steve Garvey, of course, is the first baseman for the Los Angeles Dodgers, a man who from 1974 through 1977, has put together four consistently outstanding baseball seasons—seasons that would be tough to match anywhere in the majors. Over that period Steve has averaged 644 at bats and 200 hits per season. His batting average for the period is .311. He has hit 85 home runs and collected 401 RBI's.

Along the way he has been the National League's

Most Valuable Player, the MVP of the All-Star Game, and has helped his club to a pair of National League pennants. That's not all. In 1976 he also set a league record by making the fewest errors for a first baseman in a season with 1500 or more total chances. Steve Garvey made just three errors.

During that time, Steve also acquired a reputation as baseball's all-American boy, a positive-thinking athlete who feels very strongly about the ideals and responsibilities that go with being a professional ballplayer. That reputation was reinforced in 1976 when Steve was honored as one of the five outstanding young men in the state by the California Jaycees and one of the ten outstanding in the entire country by the U.S. Jaycees.

When Steve talks about his team it's usually a combination of how things are and how Steve feels they should be.

"The Dodgers are a first-class organization," he has said. "Everyone is treated as if he is a member of the family, and I think that's the way it should be done.

"The team tries to draft players and develop them together in the minor leagues until they're ready to play together in the majors. There's a solid group of us who came up together on this team. And with players developed this way, instead of being thrown together through trades, I think you get a more positive-thinking situation; the players feel they really belong. It's a kind of . . . 'I grew up with these guys, we've played together as a unit' . . . that kind of thing.

"We always travel first class in our own jet, stay at the finest places, play in the finest stadiums. It's a wonderful blend. You stand back, draw all the pieces together and you couldn't play for a finer group of people."

Because of his allegiance to his team and to the sport, Garvey feels he has a public obligation all year round.

"I try to go through life with the idea that maybe a little boy or girl is looking over my shoulder, following me around. I wouldn't want to do anything physically or vocally that would take away from their growing up. I try to be a positive image. I think that's the big thing."

Thus Steve Garvey has become the new Frank Merriwell, a superstar who does it all by the book, the complete opposite of the so-called sports "anti-hero," the athlete who does things his own way and doesn't care who knows. Steve Garvey doesn't dig them, and they don't dig Steve Garvey. In fact, there were stories coming from the Dodger family as far back as 1975 that had some teammates publicly criticizing Steve's goodie-goodie role and claiming he was trying to push his philosophy onto them.

It was a ticklish situation, spurred perhaps by the fact that the Dodgers, expected to retain the National League championship they'd won in 1974, were hopelessly behind the Cincinnati Reds by midseason. To a degree, the whispers and the open statements that followed disillusioned Garvey, but he responded by playing even harder on the field and acknowledging that he wasn't about to change his ways because of the feelings of other people.

Some of the murmurings continued in '76. But once again some of the blame could be placed on the frustration of being buried once more by Cincinnati's Big Red Machine. The Dodgers were beginning to look like perennial runners-up. Then in 1977 the team got a new manager and, with him, a new life.

Tommy Lasorda was the man. He replaced veteran Walter Alston, who had managed the club since 1954.

This is not to put the rap on Alston. He retired as a very successful longtime skipper. But, to some, he was distant and aloof, a stern taskmaster who demanded, and usually got, a total effort from his players. Lasorda, on the other hand, believed in the family concept and, in effect, lived and died with his players. He was often seen openly embracing them after a big win, and crying with them after a tough loss. His presence, plus a super start, wiped out any semblance of dissension and restored harmony to the team. A manager with Lasorda's personality was what the Dodgers needed at the time.

But getting back to Garvey. Whether you think of Steve as an all-American boy or as a guy whose hair is too neat and whose views are too straight, you've still got to admit two things. One is that he is an individual, a strong personality who expresses his feelings and does his own thing. The other is that Steve Garvey can play ball.

Compactly built at 5'-10", 195 pounds, Garvey is a smart, line-drive hitter who can spray the ball to all fields. Since establishing himself as a starting player in 1974, he has proved day in and day out that he's for real. Consistency and durability are two of his finest qualities, and as the last four seasons have shown, it would be difficult to find his equal in those areas.

Garvey's approach to the game is a cerebral one: that is, he uses his head. During the 1974 World Series, for instance, the Oakland A's pitchers were constantly keeping the ball away from the Dodger hitters. Most of the L.A. batters took up the challenge and continued to try to pull and as a consequence, floundered badly. Not Garvey. He saw what was happening and quickly adjusted his short, compact swing. The result was eight hits, more than any other player on either team, and a .381 batting average in five games.

Steve Garvey has been a winner for a long time. In fact, listing his achievements from Little League days on makes it look as if things always came easy. But he had to work, and for a while, it even looked as if he was destined to be nothing more than a major league utility player. But once given the opportunity, Steve Garvey made the most of it.

Garvey was born on December 22, 1948, in Tampa, Florida. His full name, Steven Patrick Garvey, bespeaks his Irish origins. His family was always a close-knit one, and his parents had a lot of pride in their only child. Steve's father, Joe Garvey was a good athlete. He had been a first baseman on local and semi-pro teams and had played some minor league football on Long Island before the family moved to Tampa. Even Steve's mother, Mildred, was athletic, having played a great deal of field hockey as a youngster.

Mildred Garvey remembers kidding with Steve because she was always more limber than he was. "He'd get mad at me because he couldn't get his foot up on this counter we had," she recalls. "I'd ask him to put his foot up on the counter like mine was, and he couldn't do it."

Steve's childhood was happy. Both his parents were easygoing and affable. There was a lot of laughter in the Garvey household. Steve played ball with his father and friends from an early age, and he soon found he was in the right place for a prospective ballplayer. Florida was the training ground for most of the major league teams, and there were always spring exhibition games going on in Tampa. Steve's father was a driver for the Greyhound Company and often transported the teams out to the ball park. He sometimes took young Steve along and pretty soon Steve was serving as a bat boy for several clubs, including the Dodgers, Yankees, and Tigers. It wasn't long before the Dodgers were his favorites.

In those days the Dodgers were a National League power. The team had dominated the league in the early-to-mid-1950s, when it was located in Brooklyn. In fact, they were still the Brooklyn Dodgers when Steve first met them; they moved to Los Angeles before the 1958 season, when Steve was just nine.

The Dodgers had many stars then—Robinson, Hodges, Snider, Campanella, Furillo, Reese, Newcombe, Gilliam, Cox. They were almost household names, especially after they finally won their first World Series in 1955. It was almost inevitable that the Dodgers would be Steve's favorites, and that Gil Hodges would be his favorite person. Steve remembers those days well.

"Gil Hodges was a gentleman on and off the field. I always admired him. He always took time to play catch with me or say a kind word. And his handshake is something I'll never forget.

"There were all kinds of good memories of the Dodgers, like the time they were playing in Bradenton [Florida], and Carl Furillo was in right field in water up to his ankles. He couldn't have enjoyed it, but he stayed in there. I just had the feeling that the Dodgers were a fine bunch of men playing with a fine team, and they never did anything to change that image.

"I was bat boy for the Yankees and Tigers to some degree, too, but a few of the players on the Yankees weren't quite what I expected. When you have an idol, you always expect they're perfect. You hear them say a few cuss words, or see them refuse to sign a few autographs, and it takes some of the shine off."

So even as a young boy, Steve had a good idea how

a professional athlete should be, and he apparently
saw more of these qualities in the Dodgers than in any
other team with which he was associated.

Steve wasn't only a spectator then. At about the
same time as he became a bat boy, he also became a
Little League star. His final Little League season saw
him hit .750, with 18 home runs in 20 games. That's
three hits in every four trips to the plate. Then Steve
moved on to the Pony League. In the first four innings
of his very first game he hit for the cycle (single, double, triple, home run). Steve remembers how little
things like that were always happening to him.

"It all began to add up and make me think, 'Maybe
I am destined to be a professional athlete.'"

He was certainly thinking in terms of the major
leagues:

"We had about eleven grapefruit trees in our
backyard, and in the spring I'd take the little hard
grapefruits that had fallen off and hit them with a
broomstick. I'd pretend I was the Dodgers, and I'd im-
itate all their players. I remember even hitting line
drives back then, with the grapefruits."

Much of the credit for Steve's hitting success is his
compact build, which allows for that quick, short,
compact hitting stroke. And much of the strength in
the stroke comes from a set of thick, muscular
forearms. These, too, were developed in those early
years.

"I built up my arms by swinging a barbell as a
bat," Steve says. "And sometimes I'd use one of the
Dodgers broken bats. They were too heavy for me,
but they made me strong in the arms for my age, from
the elbows down, and that's the key to hitting."

Steve hit wherever he played, right into high school
and American Legion ball. He was also a football star
by then, a running back and defensive back who

could pop through a hole or on defense pop a runner with gusto. He liked the gridiron almost as well as the diamond, and he excelled on both playing fields.

When he thinks back to his development as an athlete, Steve credits his coaches, and his own levelheaded philosophy, for his success.

"I've always been pleased with good coaches," he said, "all the way down the line through to the pros. Now I don't mean they were all the most knowledgeable coaches in the world, but they would still help me in some way to be a better baseball player, and I think that's a big reason for my success.

"Sometimes it was just the guidance I needed as a young player. I know I always listened as much as possible and tried to do the things I was instructed to do. Gradually, as I came to know myself better, I found out the things I was best suited for. All youngsters should try to do this. Anyway, after that, as I continued to grow, I tried to work on all the basic things, the basics of fielding, hitting the ball, and running the bases. Those basics can lay a good foundation for you to work on as you get older and begin to experiment with different things.

"I always tried to be an all-around ballplayer, both defensively and offensively, and a good thinking ballplayer as well. It pays off in the long run. Consistency is another thing that pays off. To be able to go out there each day and contribute something toward the success of the team is all anyone can ask of you."

By the time he reached high school he was a big star, one the scouts and recruiters were already watching closely. On the football field he had switched to quarterback, where his talents as a runner and a passer could be used best. In his senior year his gridiron record showed more than 1,000 yards gained running and more than 1,000 yards gained passing. It was quite a performance. Playing for his dream team, the Dodgers, was in the back of Steve's mind all along; but when he was offered a football scholarship to Michigan State University, he decided to take it.

Steve played both sports for the Spartans as a freshman, then in the autumn of his sophomore year he won a starting job as a defensive back on the varsity. That, in itself, is quite a tribute to Steve's ability, since Michigan State is in the Big Ten Conference, one of the best and most highly competitive in the country.

But Steve's Michigan State career didn't really last long. Shortly after the football season ended, the major leagues held its annual player draft, plucking youngsters from college campuses all around the country. Unlike football, the baseball draft does not have to wait until a youngster's class has graduated. And in 1968, Steve was drafted by none other than the Los Angeles Dodgers.

Steve promptly left Michigan State for the career that he'd always wanted, that of a professional baseball player—a Dodger. Of course, Garvey wasn't one to turn his back on education; he continued his studies in the off-season.

Being the top draft choice for the team of his choice was a big thrill, but Steve soon found he had to make some physical adjustments because of his preparation for football at Michigan State.

"A defensive back has a rough job," he said. "Most defensive backs aren't real big, but they've got to be strong because on running plays, for instance, I always had to take out the pulling guard and tackle. To build up for that, for taking out guys that weighed maybe 240 or 250, I had to work on the weights. So I had some pretty tight muscles and a football neck. When I gave up football for good and went into baseball, I quickly realized that I had to debulk, to stretch out all those muscles. It sounds easy, but when I look back I find that it took me about three years to get my body to the point that I wanted it, to stretch out all the right muscles and keep my strength in the right places. It's interesting, the way you have to control your body for the various sports."

To listen to Steve tell it, you'd think that he was a muscle-bound oaf his first couple of years in the Dodger organization. To him, maybe, but not to the casual observer or the record. The Dodgers sent him to Ogden, Utah, for the remainder of the 1968 season and in 62 games he batted .338, with 20 homers and 59 RBIs. It was apparent to everyone that they had a potentially fine hitter in the youngster from Tampa. Steve already had the quick bat and level swing, and he hung liners all over the field.

But Steve's field work was a different story. Steve was essentially a third baseman when he joined the Dodger organization, and he figured that was the place he'd play if and when he made it to the majors. But playing the hot corner was never easy for him. He knew immediately that he'd never be another Brooks Robinson. Throwing was a particular problem. He had separated a shoulder during freshman football at Michigan State, and while the injury wasn't a bad one, it seemed to have left him with something of a scatter arm. His throwing was erratic and unpredictable, and he'd often find himself flinging the ball over the first baseman's head or scaling it in the dirt well in front of the bag. His only consolation was that he was still in the low minors, probably a couple of years away from the parent club. He hoped that hard work and a lot of throwing would straighten it out.

The next year, 1969, Steve was at Albuquerque, New Mexico, where his strong bat once again did most of his talking. Despite a broken hand, which kept him out of the lineup for a couple of months, he still managed to hit .373 in 83 games. He had 14 homers and a very impressive total of 85 RBI's, a ratio that couldn't be ignored. The Dodgers even gave the youngster a brief taste of the majors that year, bringing him up at the tail end of the season for three games. Steve had a single in three trips to the plate and the thrill of major league action for the first time. But his fielding, if nothing else, dictated a bit more seasoning in the minors.

This time it was at Spokane of the Pacific Coast League, the Dodgers top farm club, and Steve responded with a .319 average in 95 games, once again proving himself a big run producer with 15 homers and 87 RBI's. His hitting earned him a longer stint with the Dodgers. He was in 34 games with L.A. that year, being used as a pinch hitter and part-time third baseman. He came to bat 95 times, with 25 hits and a .269 average. Not bad, though his power fell off noticeably. He produced just a single home run (his first in the majors) and drove in but six runs, a sorry total, especially for the intense Garvey, who knew that hitting would have to be his ticket to a major league job.

"The fielding was coming very slowly. My arm was still wild. I couldn't always control my throws, and I was beginning to wonder whether I ever would on a regular basis. I've always been a bug on consistency and suddenly, in the field, it was the one thing I lacked. I knew I didn't have to be spectacular, but consistency was a must. So I dug in and worked harder."

In one sense, Steve came into the Dodger organization at the right time. Since the early 1940s, the Dodgers had usually been around the top of the league. There were pennants in 1941, 1947, 1949, 1952, 1953; a world championship in 1955 (their first); pennants in 1956 and 1959 (their first in Los Angeles); world championships in 1963 and 1965, and a pennant in 1966. That's 11 pennants and 3 World Series wins in a 25-year span, a hard total to top.

Of course, during some of the interim years, there had to be rebuilding programs. The teams of the late forties and the fifties featured the Dodgers that Steve first met in Tampa, the Hodges-Snider-Reese-Campanella-Furillo-Newcombe-Robinson-Gilliam teams that were as good as any. Then, in the 1960s, the club featured the likes of Sandy Koufax and Don Drysdale on the mound, Maury Wills, Tommy and Willie Davis, John Roseboro, and it got by on pitching and speed. Koufax retired with a bad elbow after the 1966 season, while some of the others began to fade. So it was time to rebuild again.

The Dodger skipper through both of the preceding eras was Walter Alston, who joined the team in 1954. Alston remembers the old Dodger teams well.

"The club when I joined it in 1954 was pretty much of a powerhouse," he recalls. "We had half a dozen guys who could reach the fence with no trouble. Playing in Ebbets Field [the team's ancient and smallish ball park in Brooklyn] helped, too. Add some good pitchers, and it was definitely a great ball club.

"In the sixties we had great pitching with Sandy and Don, pretty good defense, and concentrated speed in Wills and Willie Davis. So that club relied on its pitching, the stolen base, hit and run, squeeze plays, and stuff like that. We were in a big ball park in L.A. and were mainly a singles hitting team. We had to do it that way, but it worked.

Times had also changed as far as rebuilding a team

was concerned, and Manager Alston talked about these differences, as well:

"In 1954, the Dodgers had a veteran team that was soon to begin fading. But the farm system was excellent in those days, very strong, and it didn't take too long to replace a Campanella with a Roseboro, a Reese with a Wills.

"But by the time that club began to fade in the late sixties, the farm system had changed. Now we had the draft and couldn't sign ballplayers at random, so it took a bit longer to rebuild. The Dodgers have always tried to develop their own players rather than trade for them, and we had to watch the farms very closely."

That's where Steve Garvey came in. He was among a group of youngsters coming onto the horizon from 1969 to 1971. Steve's first full year with the Dodgers was 1971, and it turned into one of the most frustrating of his career. He was a part-time player, and for the first time ever, he didn't really hit well; his average floundered around the .225 mark all season long.

Oddly enough, Steve had been the Dodger's opening-day third baseman in both 1970 and 1971. In 1970, he was soon returned to the minors, and in 1971 he was sent to the bench. His fielding was as erratic as ever, and when his hitting fell off, then there wasn't really much left.

Dodger fans were also getting anxious. Since that last pennant in 1966, the team had fallen to eighth and then seventh before the start of divisional play in 1969. They were fourth in the Western Division that year, then second in 1970. They seemed to be on the rise and the fans wanted a winner. That's one reason the boos came hard and fast when Steve Garvey's erratic arm went to work at third.

The second half of the 1971 season was a disaster for Steve. The team had improved and was headed toward a winning record, though no championship. But Steve was on the bench. Except for an occasional pinch-hitting assignment or spot start, he rarely played. He was nervous about another demotion to the minors, or worse yet, the possibility that his beloved Dodgers would trade him. After all, he hadn't really done anything to prove he could be a consistent, positive addition to the ball club. Steve recalls that bad time and a phone call that helped keep his courage up.

"The last half of the 1971 season I was in a very insecure position," he said. "Then, one night, I received a long distance call and heard my father's voice from Florida on the other end of the line. He said, 'I know this is the lowest point in your career. But remember, we love you and we're behind you one hundred percent. You're the model son.' When you hear words like that, you ask yourself, 'Can I be that bad off?'"

So Steve hung in there, though 1971 was not the kind of season to look back on with too much fondness. In 81 games Steve hit just .227, the lowest average of his professional life. He had just 7 homers and 26 RBI's, and he made a host of errors in the field. He knew he'd never be a regular with that kind of production.

Shortly after the season ended, Steve married his college sweetheart. Then Steve and Cyndy Garvey left for the Caribbean, not for a honeymoon, but so that Steve could play winter ball and try to improve his fielding.

He wasn't in the starting lineup when 1972 began, and Steve now feared his chance might never come, at least not with the Dodgers. He assumed they were thinking of him strictly as a utility player. Bill Grabarkewitz, who had finished 1971 strongly by subbing for Wills at shortstop, was given third base. He was considered a solid fielder and had hit well enough at the end of 1971 to merit a chance.

So Steve sat on the bench again and waited. This time around Grabarkewitz didn't hit a lick, and Garvey began getting into the lineup. But he never stayed long; his fielding and throwing still kept him from a regular job. As soon as he'd uncork a wild one, the fans would jump down his throat. Even his improved hitting didn't make much of a difference.

Steve was also learning just how nasty sports "fans" could be. He was booed mercilessly. He also began receiving mail that was not only highly critical of his play but malicious and profane enough to be called "hate mail." He and Cyndy also began receiving phone calls that further berated him.

"I had to keep telling myself they were mad at the Dodger third baseman, not at Steve Garvey personally," he said. "Eventually you just have to tell them you can't talk to someone so irrational and then you have to hang up!"

Steve got into 96 games in 1972, as the Dodgers finished third in the Western Division with an 85-70 mark. His batting average was up from the year before at .269, but he had just 9 homers and 30 RBIs in 297 at bats. And he wasn't left in the lineup long enough to put anything together. How long could this kind of thing continue? So it was more winter ball and another effort to make himself into an adequate third sacker. Yet when the 1973 season began, Steve was once again on the bench, this time with a reacquired veteran, Ken McMullen at third.

The Dodger rebuilding program had also shifted gears. Several of the players who had come up around the same time as Garvey were no longer being counted on to bring the Dodgers back to the top. Youngsters like Ted Sizemore, Bill Sudakis, Bobby

Valentine, Bill Grabarkewitz, and Jim Lefebvre were either traded or sitting on the bench. Some, such as Bill Russell and Davey Lopes, were changing position (they came from the outfield to take over at short and second). And another youngster, Ron Cey, was being groomed for a shot at third. Bill Buckner was playing first, but he could also play the outfield; while two new catchers, Joe Ferguson and Steve Yaeger, were also on hand. And Steve Garvey began to wonder if he, too, was being phased out.

It became more acute when McMullen bowed out at third and was immediately replaced by Cey. Alston had as much as said that the job was Cey's as long as he could keep it, and Cey was keeping it on an everyday basis.

The first two months of the 1973 season became a new low-point in Steve Garvey's career. He had started in less than a dozen games that year and was batting .228.

"It was the definite low-point," he recalls. "With each passing day it began to look more and more as if Cey was the third baseman. He wasn't about to be moved out. I was hardly playing at all, just pinch hitting occasionally and sometimes not getting in for two weeks because I didn't have a position. I was really starting to get down. But finally I just said to myself, if I'm ever going to get anywhere with this team, I've just got to do it when the opportunity comes—any opportunity."

So Steve dug in, and the next time Manager Alston called on him to pinch hit, he went up to the plate with more concentration and determination than ever before. Pinch hitting isn't easy. A player comes up cold: he hasn't been in the game and the mucles aren't limber. Not everyone can do it. Even some of the game's best hitters have been repeatedly frustrated when called upon to be pinch swingers. When Steve went up there he just tried to isolate his concentration on the pitcher, as he would if he were a regular. He promptly smashed a solid single to left.

From that point on, Steve became a pinch hitter extraordinaire. He banged out 10 hits in 24 pinch-hitting situations, and that's a .417 clip. His hits weren't cheapies either; they were solid line drives, many coming in clutch spots with the game on the line. Even a good number of his outs were on solid shots. He was making contact with consistency, and people in the Dodger camp were taking notice.

The problem was what to do with him. Ron Cey was asserting himself at third. He was showing fine potential at the plate and a consistency in the field. So to reinsert Garvey at third was out. In fact, there were young players at almost every position. Yet some kind of decision had to be made. By all the evidence, including his latest pinch-hitting spree, Steve Garvey had what it takes to be a fine major league batter. Finally, Alston came up with a solution.

In 1970 and 1971, another young ballplayer named Bill Buckner has been an outfield starter. Then, in 1972, with the retirement of all-star first baseman, Wes Parker, Buckner had come in and played first. This was because the Dodgers had acquired outfielder Frank Robinson in a trade. Buckner was again at first when 1973 began, but Robinson had been traded away and there was an outfield spot open if Alston wanted to move him. Without warning, Alston told Buckner he'd be returning to left, where he was outstanding, and he handed a first-baseman's mitt to Steve Garvey.

"I want you in there every day," he told Garvey. "And we feel you'll be able to do the job at first."

At first Steve was dumbfounded. He had played

some first base during his career, but not in the majors, and he never really considered himself a first baseman. But with characteristic determination, he took the glove and immediately began learning about the new position (the same position played by his early idol, Gil Hodges).

Some people consider first an easy position, a dumping ground for players who can't cut it anywhere else. For years, first base has been a kind of preservation ground for aging outfielders, so they can save their legs for hitting. Mickey Mantle, Willie Mays, and Henry Aaron all played some first base in the latter stages of their careers, but none of them found it an easy task!

It's one thing to play first base, and it's another to play it well. It's more than just catching the ball. Neither Mantle, Mays, nor Aaron, for instance, was ever really comfortable at first. Aaron, for one, asked to return to the outfield. In fact, the only all-star outfielder who has become an all-star-caliber first baseman late in his career has been the Red Sox Carl Yastrzemski. And Yaz is just a fielding natural.

There had to be question marks both in Steve Garvey's mind and in the minds of the Dodger brass when the stocky youngster went out to first base with no practical experience. For one thing, managers like first basemen to be tall and rangy, so they can go up for those high throws and stretch out for the close ones. When you think of a typical first baseman a player like Willie "Stretch" McCovey comes to mind. His lanky, 6'-4" frame has turned many potential wild throws and close plays into outs. Many thought that Garvey, at 5'-10", was too short to play the position effectively.

Garvey had plenty of help from Buckner and the Dodger coaches, and he concentrated on learning the footwork and other skills needed around the bag. Fortunately, he didn't let it affect his hitting. He immediately went on a tear that saw him hit safely in nine of his first ten games. The hits came in bunches, two or three to a game, raising his batting average up over the .300 mark in a matter of weeks. And he was doing a nice job at first. The experiment was working.

To the surprise of many, Steve was making one of the most difficult aspects of playing first—digging low throws out of the dirt—look easy. Some players can never do it well, but Steve was scooping them out as if he had been doing it all his life. He was also showing a remarkable ability to recover and make sweep tags on plays that saw him pulled off the bag, and this compensated somewhat for his lack of height and reach. Because of this, he had perhaps more collisions at first than most first sackers, but this didn't bother him at all. After all, as an ex-football player, he was used to contact. Dodger Coach Monty Basgall, who was helping and observing Steve constantly during this period of transition, often marveled at the tenacity with which Steve went after charging base runners.

"He's not afraid of any physical thing in the world," the coach said.

As for Steve, he was overjoyed with everything. He was finally getting the chance to play, was hitting very well, and gathering additional confidence with each passing game. For the first time since coming up to the Dodgers, he felt he would remain in the lineup, that he had finally found a place for himself.

"I think first base is more my natural position," Steve told reporters. "In the past most of my errors have been throwing errors and not fielding errors, and I really haven't had any major problems adjusting.

The nice thing is that Manager Alston agrees about it, too."

With Steve's run-producing bat in the lineup every day, the Dodgers resumed their chase of the front-running Cincinnati Reds in the National League's Western Division. It was a young Dodger team on the field now, and many observers felt they had a good chance to catch the Reds in 1973, and if not, they would definitely be a factor in the ensuing seasons. Ferguson and Yaeger continued to split the catching duties; Garvey was at first; the speedy, base-stealing Davey Lopes was at second; the improving Bill Russell was at short; and steady Ron Cey was at third. The outfield now consisted of Buckner in left; veteran Willie Davis in center; and another youngster, Willie Crawford, in right. Alston also had some veteran reserves with whom he could platoon or replace if necessary.

Only the pitching was suspect. Newly acquired Andy Messersmith, veteran Don Sutton, and veteran Tommy John were the principal starters. Another reliable starter or two was needed. The bullpen was dependable, if not spectacular, but as Alston himself had said:

"Our team in the late fifties was pretty much of a powerhouse, while our title teams of the sixties did it with speed and pitching. This club is probably the best balanced of all."

It was Steve Garvey, to a large degree, who provided the final cog in the wheel of balance. For the remainder of the 1973 season Garvey gave the club something he had striven for since coming up. He was consistent not only at the plate but also in the field. He kept his average above the .300 mark for the entire second half of the season, hitting consistently and driving in runs. He was playing every day for the first time in his career and was improving at first with each passing game. In fact, he was becoming an outstanding first baseman, something which even the most optimistic of Dodgers had not expected.

The Dodgers played very well during the second half of 1973, but Cincy kept up its hot pace. Although Los Angeles finished with a 95-66 record, their best since 1965, they finished second in their division to the Reds. Yet the future augured very well for L.A.

The future also looked bright for Garvey. He completed his best and most satisfying season ever by hitting .304, the best on the team among the players participating in more than 100 games. He had wound up playing in 114, banging out 106 hits in 349 at bats, including 8 homers and 50 RBI's. He had also 17 doubles and 3 triples.

When the season was over, someone asked Garvey about his sudden success. Of course, a great deal of it was triggered by the fact that he played every day, but the articulate Garvey saw it as something more as well.

"I guess the difference would be intensity and concentration," he said. "I've learned to block out everything else when I get out onto the field. It's so important to be able to concentrate. You just can't succeed when your mind is wandering.

"It's rough enough to hit a baseball, you know, a round ball and a round bat, and you've got to hit it square. You just can't do it consistently unless your concentration is complete. The same goes in the field. You've got to be concentrating on every situation, so you know exactly what to do without hesitation. Otherwise, you'll lose that important split second, or you'll blow the play completely.

"So I think the difference between a really successful athlete and an athlete who has the same ability but who only performs to the average level is dedication, intensity, and concentration."

When Steve came to the Dodger camp in Florida to begin the 1974 season, he came with a new feeling of security. He had a job, and what is more, the Dodgers seemed ready to make a real run for the National League pennant. The club had made two key trades which they hoped would put them over the top. They first brought center fielder Jim Wynn from Houston. Wynn, a diminutive slugger, had had some personal problems while playing for the Astros. The Dodgers figured he would add power to their attack. Then they took their previous centerfielder, Willie Davis, and traded him to Montreal for relief pitcher Mike Marshall. Marshall was an effective fireman with one exceptional quality. He had a tireless arm and could pitch nearly every day if called upon. In fact, he had set a major league record by appearing in 92 games for the Expos in 1973 and had indicated he wanted to work even more in 1974.

The Dodgers started the season with a bang, winning early and winning big. It seemed as if everyone was hitting. Wynn was particularly conspicuous in his new surroundings, as he jumped atop the league in homers and RBI's. There were also major contributions from Buckner, Russell, Lopes, and Cey, as well as Garvey, who was stinging the ball as well as he had at the end of 1973. He wasn't getting much notice, however, because of Wynn's flashy start.

By the end of May the Dodgers were really rolling. They already had a seven-game lead over Cincinnati and were pacing both leagues in almost every major batting and pitching category.

Wynn, known as the "Toy Cannon," led the league in homers with 12 and in RBI's with 37. His batting average was up around the .330 mark. Left fielder Buckner was carrying on at about .340, while Willie Crawford, Russell, and Cey were all in the .290's. As for Steve, he had silently crept up to number two in homers with 8 and was hitting around .320. Before the year was out, his consistency would overshadow all the rest.

The club was also getting good pitching, especially from starters Messersmith and Sutton and from reliever Marshall, who was proving to be all that was said about him. He was pitching well and at a pace that seemed to target him for a 100-game season. It was hard to conceive of anyone pitching that often, but then again, everything was going right for the Dodgers. That sentiment was quickly echoed by Manager Alston.

"Sure, I'll admit things have gone just right for us," he said. "We've won a few that maybe we shouldn't have, but we've also been working hard to stay one step ahead of our opponents. This is a very sound ball club. Just look at it this way. We won ninety-five games last year with a bunch of inexperienced kids, and that year of experience is really paying off this time around."

Experience plus newcomers Wynn and Marshall and the full-time services of Steve Garvey were the ingredients that made the difference. Garvey was quickly proving that the second half of the 1973 season was no fluke.

He was becoming the steadying influence on the team, as his consistency went unmatched throughout the year. His average was above .300 all season long, and he never went more than three games without getting a hit. His line drives were producing runs at an impressive clip, and his fielding at first was better than ever.

As midseason approached, the Dodgers were still first by a comfortable margin. Now the All-Star game was coming up and the fans began filing their votes for the starters. The latest method for electing the starting team was for the fans to obtain a printed ballot from the league. The ballot was broken down by positions, and under each position were the names of the players most likely to be candidates, in other words, the five or six men considered the best at their respective positions. Because he was still a virtual unknown when the ballots were printed, Garvey's name wasn't on it.

There is a provision for write-in votes on the ballot, but the fans usually find it easier to put a check next to a name rather than write one in. That makes it doubly difficult for a player to make the team via the write-in route. So Steve's expectations weren't too high.

Fortunately, baseball fans can be a knowledgeable lot. There are surely times when they'll vote for a perennial favorite, a tried veteran, instead of a "hot" player. But in Steve's case they saw the light. The write-in votes began coming in in droves—by the hundreds, the thousands, the hundreds of thousands. When the final tally was in, Steve Garvey had made the National League All-Star team by virtue of more than a million write-in votes.

"This is obviously the thrill of a lifetime for me," Steve said. "I didn't think it was possible. It's another one of my boyhood dreams come true, and I never thought it would happen like this or so quickly. I hope I don't let the fans down."

He didn't. In the true Frank Merriwell tradition, Steve was not only in the game, he dominated it. Using that short, compact swing against unsuspecting American League pitchers, he crashed out two key hits and then made a diving stop in the field to choke off an A.L. threat. The National League had still another All-Star win, and Steve Garvey received a trophy as the game's Most Valuable Player. It was rapidly becoming a storybook season for him.

The second half of the year continued to show that Garvey was no fluke. In fact, during that second half, he began to emerge as the field leader of the Dodgers. A nagging injury slowed Wynn's pace while Buckner, Cey, Lopes, and Russell all had their streaky spots. But Garvey was like the Rock of Gibraltar. Day in and day out he was in the lineup and contributing. He was batting fourth now, the clean-up spot. While he wasn't the classic slugger, he was getting the job done, taking over from Wynn as the club RBI leader and staying up among the league's best. He was the man the Dodgers knew they could depend on to get the job done.

He was also becoming one of the most popular Dodgers in other ways. Remembering how he felt as a youngster when a player like Gil Hodges spoke with him and signed an autograph, Steve tried to relate to youngsters in the same way. He knew there were athletes who didn't give autographs, but he felt he had an obligation to the fans. He was representing not only himself, but the Dodger organization and baseball as a whole. So whenever possible he signed and gave a friendly, smiling word to youngsters and fans of all ages.

No one could blame Steve, of course, for being a happy man. He was putting the wraps on a great season and the Dodgers were putting the wraps on the Western Division title, taking it with relative ease after leading all the way. And when it ended, people began to realize just how great a season Steve Garvey had had.

The rough figures read this way: .312 batting average, 21 home runs, 111 runs batted in, 200 hits, 95 runs scored. In the field Steve Garvey made just eight errors all year, earning him the Gold Glove Award as the best fielder in the league at his position. Not bad for an error-prone infielder. But his hitting was the big thing, and most people figured it would be needed as the Dodgers went up against the Pittsburgh Pirates in a three of five series for the National League pennant.

If the Los Angeles team had any weaknesses, they were on the mound, where there were just two reliable starters in Messersmith (20 wins) and Sutton (19). But the club had Mike Marshall, who had set an unbelievable major league record by appearing in 106 of the Dodgers 162 games, pitching 208⅓ innings of relief (winning 15 and saving 21). He was soon to become the first relief pitcher ever to win the Cy Young Award. The Dodgers figured they'd need Marshall against the Pirates, which was one of the best hitting teams in baseball.

Yet the pitching was better than the Dodgers expected. Sutton, who had won 13 of his last 14 decisions in the regular season shut out the Pirates in the first game, 3-0. In the second game Messersmith and Marshall combined for a 5-2 Los Angeles win. Pittsburgh bounded back to take the third, but Sutton returned to the mound for the fourth game, which was played before nearly 55,000 fans in Los Angeles.

Steve had been relatively quiet in the first three games, coming through with a couple of singles, but not doing anything spectacular. But the fourth game was all his. Wynn doubled home a Dodger run in the first. Then in the third with two out, Wynn walked. Up came Steve, facing left-hander Jerry Reuss. Reuss tried to keep the ball away from the right-handed batting Garvey, but Garvey went with the pitch and sent a liner to right center. It wasn't a towering drive, but the power behind it carried it over the wall for a two-run homer. The Dodgers led 3-0.

Then in the fifth, Wynn walked again. This time left-hander Ken Brett was on the mound. He tried to curve Garvey, and this time the liner was pulled to left. Again it cleared the wall for another two-run homer. It gave the Dodgers a 5-0 lead and just about put the game on ice.

The Dodgers just rolled it up after that, winning the game and the pennant, 12-1, as Steve had two more hits and wound up with a .389 average for the four-game series. Now the Dodgers were World Series bound. They would meet the Oakland A's, a team that had won the world's championship the previous two seasons.

In the A's, the Dodgers would be facing a team that was in many ways similar, but in many ways their opposite. Both were California based, making for the first "freeway" series, but while the Dodgers were generally considered as one big happy family, the A's were involved in more battles than Napoleon.

Known as the Fighting A's, the club was constantly in turmoil. Players were ever at odds with flamboyant owner Charles O. Finley, and almost all of the team's stars were either taking pot shots at Finley in the press or asking to be traded. During the 1973 series, which the A's won from the New York Mets, the players threatened to boycott when Finley dismissed a utility player, Mike Andrews, because he had made two errors in a crucial game. And when they weren't fighting with Finley, they were battling among themselves. Right before the start of the 1974 classic, there was a clubhouse brawl between pitchers Blue Moon Odom and Rollie Fingers. It wasn't the first time those kinds of shenanigans had gone on.

But despite this the team was loaded with top talent, such as pitcher Catfish Hunter (who was suing Finley for breach of contract and eventually became a free agent), Vida Blue (who once held out for over a month to protest Finley's contract offer), and Ken Holtzman (who perennially threatened retirement as a protest over Finley's actions).

The other players were just as notable. Outfielder Reggie Jackson (the biggest Finley baiter of them all) was considered the team's top slugger and superstar. Outfielder Joe Rudi, third baseman Sal Bando, first sacker Gene Tenace, and shortstop Bert Campaneris were other top players who had contributed to Series victories over the Cincinnati Reds and New York Mets. The A's were no team to mess with, yet for some reason the Dodgers were solid favorites when the fall classic began.

Lefty Holtzman was facing Messersmith in game one, played in Los Angeles. The A's struck first when right fielder Jackson, hobbled by a pulled hamstring muscle, stroked one over the left field wall. Then in the fifth, pitcher Holtzman doubled, went to third on a wild pitch, and scored when Campaneris executed a perfect suicide squeeze bunt. The final Oakland run came in the eighth on a single, sacrifice, and wild throw by third baseman Cey. The Dodgers got one back in the fifth on a pair of Oakland errors and another on a Wynn homer in the ninth. Garvey followed Wynn's homer with a single, but then Catfish Hunter came out of the bullpen to strike out Joe Ferguson to end the game. Oakland had won it, 3-2.

Sutton pitched the Dodgers back into it with a 3-2 win of his own in game two. The first run came in off Vida Blue on a walk and two singles, the next two on a single by Garvey and homer by Ferguson. But that wasn't all Garvey contributed to the victory.

With one out in the Oakland eighth, pinch hitters Jim Holt and Claudell Washington smacked back-to-back singles. An error by Russell on a Campaneris grounder loaded the bases with speedy Bill North at bat.

North hit a sharp grounder up the middle. Shortstop Russell cut it off, stepped on second, and fired to first, hoping for a double play. The ball was low, bounding in the dirt several feet in front of the stretching Garvey. But Steve stayed cool, as he had all year. With a sweeping motion of his glove he scooped the ball up in time to nip North. The rally was over.

"It was the key play of the game," said the A's Sal Bando. "If he doesn't catch that ball, we have two runs and a man on second."

But Steve was used to low throws. "I'm not as tall as most first basemen," he said, "and I think my infielders are in fear of throwing over my head. So they're more conscious of keeping the ball down and consequently throw in the dirt quite often. I must have had thirty or thirty-five of those pickups this year, and I'm getting pretty much accustomed to it."

So the series was tied at one and still a toss-up. But no one was prepared for what would happen in the next three games. In fact, one Dodger made the mistake of berating the A's before the third game. He said:

"We won 104 games during the season; they won 88. And they look to me like an 88-game club."

It wasn't the wisest thing in the world to say, especially when Oakland's postseason play had been so good the past two years. As is usually the case, someone pinned a copy of the remarks in the Oakland clubhouse, and they used it to fire themselves up before the remaining games.

For the remainder of the Series the A's played brilliantly in the field, while the Dodgers began looking more and more like a bunch of inexperienced youngsters. It was Al Downing against Catfish Hunter in game three. The A's got two in the third when catcher Joe Ferguson made a pair of errors and one more in the fourth. The Dodgers got single tallies in the eighth and ninth on homers by Buckner and Crawford, but the game ended at 3-2.

Game four was pivotal, and in a special sense, a game Steve Garvey would never forget. It wasn't his hitting he'd remember, though he was the only Dodger making good contact on a regular basis. In fact, it wasn't even the result of the game that would stick in his memory. In the early innings, Garvey learned that his wife had given birth to a daughter, Krisha Lee Garvey. He said he was "trying to hit one for Krisha" that day, but he had to settle for a couple of solid singles. Unfortunately, there was little help from his Dodger mates.

The A's went ahead 1-0 on a homer by pitcher Holtzman. Then the Dodgers took a 2-1 lead when Garvey singled, Ferguson walked, and Russell cracked a triple between a drawn-in outfield. But Andy Messersmith couldn't hold the lead. In the sixth the A's rallied, scored four times, and held on for a 5-2 victory. They now led three games to one, and the Dodgers seemed all but finished.

Neither team was really powdering the ball, but the A's (especially their second baseman, Dick Green) were fielding beautifully. Green made several miraculous stops which he turned into double plays ending Dodger rallies. So not even the breaks were working for L.A.

It was Sutton versus Blue in game five—the A's trying to wrap it up, the Dodgers trying to stave off defeat. In the first inning the A's Bill North tried to steal second and catcher Yaeger promptly threw the ball into centerfield. A sacrifice fly by Sal Bando made it 1-0. Then in the second, A's catcher Ray Fosse homered to make it 2-0. Dodger hopes were fading.

L.A. still had one gasp left. They got runners on second and third in the sixth. Wynn brought one home with a sacrifice fly, and then Steve drove in the tying tally with a sharp single before the A's closed out the threat. In the bottom of the seventh the Dodgers had relief ace Marshall on the mound. The game was halted temporarily as fans in the left field stands began throwing debris at left fielder Buckner. When the game resumed Joe Rudi was up. He saw that Marshall hadn't taken any warmup tosses during the delay, so he dug in for the first pitch. Sure enough, it didn't have anything on it, and Rudi belted it into the seats for a go-ahead homer.

The Dodgers had a chance to tie in the eighth when Buckner opened with a single. When the ball skipped past center fielder North, Buckner raced to second. Only he didn't stop, he gambled and headed to third. Once again the A's came through. Two perfect throws cut down the sliding Buckner and the rally was nipped right then and there. Rollie Fingers, who was to become Series MVP, retired the Dodgers in the eighth and ninth to nail down the victory. The A's had won in five games.

It was a bitter disappointment for the young Dodger team. They hadn't played well. In fact, neither team had hit much: the A's had .211; the Dodgers had .228. The leading hitter among the regulars on both teams was Steve Garvey. Steady as usual, Garvey had 8 hits in 21 at bats for a .381 average. No other Dodger regular hit above .250. One writer, in fact, called Garvey "the noblest Dodger of them all."

The gloom of losing was lifted somewhat for Steve

Garvey several weeks after the season ended. That's when he learned he had been chosen the Most Valuable Player in the National League. It was quite an honor, but it didn't come without controversy. Many people thought the prize should have gone to the great St. Louis Card veteran Lou Brock, who, at age thirty-five, had set an amazing record by stealing 118 bases during the season. Naturally, many writers asked Steve about his selection and about the way the award was given.

"As with most awards now," Steve said, "there are three or four guys who have an excellent chance, and it just depends on how the voters see it. Lou Brock is a man of integrity. I admire him. He's a great ballplayer, and I know he was let down. Anyone would be. But I think the award was voted on justly.

"Some people feel the players should pick the MVP, not the writers, since they perform alongside and opposite each other all year. But the writers are on the scene for the entire season as well. So I guess you could make an argument for each side. It's just six of one, half a dozen of the other."

The MVP prize certainly had an effect on Steve's life. There were requests for many more public appearances, some off-field endorsements (such as a public relations job for a major soft drink company), and coupled with his great season, ammunition to practically double his salary into the $90,000 range.

Steve welcomed the public appearances because he felt they gave him a chance to talk about "some of the things I believe in." That's when he got his reputation as the all-American boy. He was always clean-cut, impeccably dressed, hair short and in place. He talked only about good, positive things—the virtues of sport, of God, of America—and about the "death of the anti-hero." It allowed him to be a "twelve month a year baseball promoter." But it was these very things that began to annoy some of his teammates during the 1975 season.

It was a season of bitter disappointment for the Dodgers. To begin with, the Cincinnati Reds got off to a fast start and never slowed down, putting the Dodgers in the back seat at the start. And playing catch-up isn't very easy, as the Reds had found out the year before. Then there were the injuries. It seemed as if they came in bunches.

The team suffered nearly fifty injuries in 1975. At various times the following key players were on the shelf for extended periods: Sutton, Wynn, Marshall, Ferguson, Russell, and Buckner. Though the team finished with an 88-74 mark, they were some twenty games behind Cincinnati, which burned all year and wound up 108-54. The Dodgers were never in it, and when a team is going badly, the resentments begin to surface.

Steve saw it coming, since he was having another super season.

"There were feelings and vibrations and little remarks," he told a writer. "I just put them out of my mind because I didn't want somebody's little remark to interfere with my job. But when it came out publicly there was no more disillusioned person with professional sports than myself, because I couldn't believe anyone would say anything publicly against a teammate. It was the ultimate slap in the face. I could have handled it one-on-one if they'd come to me directly."

The remarks allegedly had to do with Steve's goodie-goodie image and his promotional zeal for his own lifestyle. One story appeared in a San Bernardino paper which claimed that several anonymous teammates resented the way Steve had been acting. There was even criticism of Steve's wife, Cyndy, for "sticking her face in front of the cameras." And one player came right out and said:

"I don't mind what Steve does. If he wants to go out of his way to be a clean-cut kid, that's fine, as long as he doesn't interfere with my style. Sometimes, he has interfered."

There were allegedly apologies at a team meeting, but some say things were never the same that year with the Dodgers.

"Steve told me he was glad in a way that it happened," Cyndy Garvey told a reporter. "It showed him how he stood with the team. In some ways it made him more secure in the way he is. He does the things he does because he is that way. He believes what he says, and he won't change to please someone else."

Steve tried to analyze and explain the problem, or what he felt it to be.

"I think there is more jealousy in a team sport than an individual sport," he said. "As a rule you have one or two people behind you for a position, and there is a competitiveness to be the best. You have a group of guys who came up with a common goal, to reach the highest level they possibly can. When they make the majors they've made it, and the next thing is to lead the team. In baseball you see what every individual does. There has to be a little jealousy or vanity for somebody who may be doing a little better.

"I think jealousy had something to do with it in this case. I don't *do* anything. I've never tried to convert anyone. Maybe sometimes my doing things, like signing autographs or making appearances, puts pressure on other guys to do the same thing. But that's not it. If you feel like doing these things, you do them. Maybe they thought I was setting an example. . . . If we got attention it was not because we asked for it. People came to us for interviews."

On the field, Steve was one of the few Dodgers to have an outstanding season. He upped his batting average to .319, tied Pete Rose for second place in the hit parade with 210 (behind Dave Cash's 213), whacked out 18 homers and drove home 95 more runs. He had another banner year in the field with just 8 errors. He was truly an all-star again and one of the young superstars of the game.

In 1976, the Dodgers vowed to overtake the Reds once again. Manager Alston indicated that it could be his final year, and the club wanted to win it for him. But it wouldn't be easy. Many people were calling the team from Cincy one of the best ever. They were loaded with talent and the Dodgers would have to put together a great season to overtake them.

Perhaps the Redlegs had some sort of jinx over the Dodgers by then, for after just a couple of months it seemed pretty obvious that the Reds would take it once again. They were the world champs and wanted to repeat.

That's just what happened. The Redlegs rolled to another divisional title, another pennant, then swamped the revamped New York Yankees in four straight to become world champs for the second consecutive time. With their awesome power, the Reds seemed to be building a dynasty.

So the situation didn't look good for the Dodgers. They still had a solid team, but another year of chasing the Reds could have well destroyed the team psychologically.

Steve was rock-solid again in '76. He got his 200 hits and batted .317, and he also set the fielding mark with just three errors. But his run production was down. He hit only 13 homers and drove in 80 runs. That was part of the Dodger problem. The team wasn't producing enough runs. Steve and third baseman Cey were the team's top run producers with 80 ribbys apiece.

Before 1977 began, the expected had happened. Manager Alston retired and Tommy Lasorda took his place. Lasorda also became the head cheerleader, preaching togetherness and positive thinking.

He didn't mince words. "Personally, I'm sick and tired of seeing another team in the Fall Classic," he said. "But it's going to take everybody pulling together—25 players, four coaches, and the manager. All pulling the rope together, not 12 guys on one side of the rope and 13 on the other. Togetherness."

Pretty soon Lasorda had the players believing in themselves. He reminded them they'd have rightfielder Reggie Smith (acquired in mid-'76) for the entire year, and then announced a trade bringing veteran centerfielder Rick Monday to the club. He also told Dusty Baker he'd be the regular leftfielder, giving the youngster's confidence a big shot in the arm. In fact, he intended to play the same men every day, eliminating the worry over who would be starting.

He did one other thing. He told Steve Garvey he thought he could provide added run production.

"With your strength and swing you should hit 30 homers a year and still get your 200 hits and .300 average," he told Steve.

Fortunately, for the Dodgers, they started like gangbusters, beating everyone in sight. At the same time the Reds were stumbling. The Big Red Machine was hitting as usual, but suddenly their pitching collapsed, and their once powerful bullpen had been decimated by trades. L.A. won 25 of its first 29 games and jumped off to a huge lead. And the Dodgers looked like the most powerful team in the majors in doing it. Lasorda's togetherness seemed to be working.

Third baseman Cey was a virtual house afire in

April. He hit everything thrown his way and led the majors in both homers and RBIs. But he had help. Outfielders Smith and Baker were both producing with regularity and would continue to do so the entire year. Plus the club was getting solid performances from the rest of the cast, catcher Steve Yeager, and the keystone combo of Bill Russell and Davey Lopes.

Only Steve Garvey was struggling, off to the slowest start in years. Perhaps it was because he was following Lasorda's advice and going for the long ball. Perhaps it was just an old-fashioned slump. At any rate, he wasn't hitting. Fortunately, the others were, so there was no real pressure on him. Steve could come out of it on his own, and there was little doubt that he would.

The Dodger steamroller continued into May and June. The club was drawing fans at a record-breaking pace. Everyone in L.A. seemed to sense this was the year. Many show-biz personalities, such as Frank Sinatra and Don Rickles, came to the games regularly and visited the locker room. Lasorda's exuberance had rubbed off on everyone.

During May and June, Cey began to level off. But, as expected, Steve Garvey began hitting. As usual, there were line drives to all fields. And, as ordered by the boss, more home runs into the far reaches of the large stadium. Steve was again doing it all.

By the All-Star break he was up among the league leaders in many offensive categories and once again voted to a starting berth on the team. In addition, he continued to be a celebrity around town, this time with no complaints from his teammates. It was the old story. When you're winning. . . .

Steve and Cyndy appeared on panel-type game shows together, plus Steve was a judge several times on the whacky "Gong Show." He also taped another special, the "Celebrity Battle of the Sexes," where he played ping pong against football sportscaster and TV personality Phyllis George. His good looks, pleasing personality, and quick wit made him a sought-after guest.

But all the while he continued to produce on the field. Though the other Dodgers were all having fine seasons, they would take turns streaking, one picking up the slack while the other dropped off. But once he found the groove, Steve Garvey was as consistent as ever, delivering big hits, driving in runs, and playing with the same drive day after day. The things he had so much wanted to achieve, consistency and durability, he had.

Cincinnati tried to catch the Dodgers, but couldn't. Their pitching just wasn't up to it. Even the acquisition of Tom Seaver from the Mets before midseason didn't help. Seaver wound up with 21 wins, but it wasn't enough to catch the front runners. L.A. was able to coast the final two months. They took the divisional title and now looked forward to meeting the powerful Philadelphia Phillies for the National League pennant.

It seemed that Lasorda's togetherness had worked, and the confidence he showed in players like Baker and Smith produced results. Smith hit .307 with 32 homers and 87 RBI's. Baker checked in at .291 with 30 homers and 86 RBI's. Cey never recovered the pace of that torrid April, but nevertheless finished with a season of 30 homers and 110 RBI's, even though his average dropped to .241.

But once again the biggest Dodger of them all was Steve Garvey. Steve followed his manager's advice and went for the long ball more often. As a result, he wound up with career highs of 33 homers and 115 runs batted in. Yet the rest of his productiveness didn't suffer. He still managed a .297 batting average with 192 hits. Off slightly, perhaps, but the added run production more than made up for it. And considering he had gotten off to a very slow start, it had to be considered another outstanding year.

If the Dodgers had any weakness it might be the pitching. Lefthander Tommy John, the man with the so-called bionic arm, which had been reconstructed through complex tendon surgery, was a 20-game winner. Rick Rhoden started fast, then faded a bit, but still won 16. Former ace Don Sutton had an off year with 14-8, yet was always a money pitcher. Doug Rau also won 14. But the bullpen was uncertain ever since knuckleball ace Charley Hough went sour just before the All-Star break.

The Phillies, on the other hand, looked like a powerhouse. Greg Luzinski drove home 130 runs, Mike Schmidt 101. And there was added hitting support from Bake McBride, Gary Maddox, Rich Hebner, and others. In fact, the team led the National League with a .279 average, and with 795 RBI's. They were second only to the Dodgers in homers.

In addition, their pitching staff was sound. Big Steve Carlton would be a Cy Young winner by virtue of his 23 wins. Young Larry Christianson won 19, and Jim Lonborg compiled an 11-4 mark after coming back from arm problems. Plus their bullpen had a righty-lefty stopper combo in Gene Garber and Tug McGraw, and an outstanding middle and long man in Ron Reed. The Phils were a solid ballclub in every phase of the game.

The best of five playoff series opened in Los Angeles with Steve Carlton facing Tommy John. The Phillies served notice in a hurry, getting two runs off John in the first. When they got two more in the fourth and one in the fifth, taking a 5-0 lead and driving out

John, it looked bleak, especially since Carlton had been sailing along without much trouble.

The Dodgers got one back in the fifth, but in the last of the seventh it was still 5-1. That's when Ron Cey did his thing. The Dodgers loaded the bases and Cey unloaded them, belting a grand slam homer and driving Carlton from the mound. The L.A. fans went wild.

Now it was a battle of the bullpens. Gene Garber was pitching for the Phils and Elias Sosa for the Dodgers. And in the top of the ninth it was the Phils who got to Sosa for a pair of runs. Tug McGraw then came in and held the Dodgers in the bottom of the inning. The Phils had a 7-5 victory and took a 1-0 lead in the series.

Steve didn't drive in any runs in the opener, but he had three hits in four trips. As usual, he was hitting when the chips were down.

In the second game, the Dodgers turned to their money pitcher, Don Sutton, and he came through. He gave up nine hits, but managed to hold the Phillies to one run. The Dodgers, on the other hand, made the most of their nine hits. Dusty Baker followed Cey's example and belted a grand slam in the fifth. Davey Lopes, Reggie Smith, and Steve Yeager drove in the other runs, and the Dodgers took it, 7-1. Then came the pivotal third game with Burt Hooten of the Dodgers facing Larry Christianson of the Phils.

This was the game everybody would remember, as the scene shifted to Philadelphia. In the second inning Steve singled and scored the first of two Dodger runs. Then the Phils quickly KO'd Hooten by coming back with three in their half of the inning. The Dodgers tied it in the fourth, but in the bottom of the eighth Philly went to work and got two more to break the tie.

Going into the ninth the Dodgers trailed by two, 5-3, and were facing Phil relief ace Gene Garber.

Garber quickly disposed with the first two Dodgers and the game seemed to be in the bag. Then Manager Lasorda sent up veteran Vic Davalillo to pinch hit. With two strikes, Davalillo bunted and beat it out! Up came another pinch-hitting vet, Manny Mota. Mota promptly blasted one to left which Luzinski trapped against the wall. It went for a double, and on a bad relay throw Davalillo scored and Mota went to second.

Suddenly the Dodger bench was alive, with Davey Lopes up. Lopes whacked one to third that caromed off Schmidt's glove to shortstop Bowa, who fired to first. But the speedy Lopes beat it out by a hair, and Mota scored the tying run. The impossible was happening. And it wasn't over yet.

Garber was worried about the steal and tried to pick Lopes off. He threw the ball past first baseman Hebner, and Lopes easily went to second where he then scored on a clutch single by Russell. The Dodgers had a 6-5 lead, which their reliever, Mike Garman, held onto. The game was over. The super comeback in Philadelphia gave L.A. a commanding 2-1 lead in the series.

The next day the Dodgers won it in fine style. Playing in a steady rain, Tommy John bested Steve Carlton, 4-1, and the Dodgers had won the pennant, the 15th for the combined Brooklyn-Los Angeles franchise.

Now came the World Series. L.A. would be meeting their old rivals, the New York Yankees. The Yanks had beaten Kansas City in a five-game playoff, winning the last game in the final inning. It was a powerful Yankee ballclub, "the best team money could buy," according to some. The Yanks had been buying players and signing free agents, and now had the likes of Don Gullett and Reggie Jackson, to go along with Catfish Hunter, Thurman Munson, Graig Nettles, Sparky Lyle, Mike Torez, Chris Chambliss, Mickey Rivers, and the rest of a strong cast. The Yanks had been beaten four straight by the Reds in the '76 Series and wanted the title very badly.

But the team had been plagued by internal dissension all year long, battles between Jackson and Munson, manager Billy Martin and owner George Steinbrenner. Plus there were some sore arms on the pitching staff, notably Hunter's, and the Dodgers were hoping all these factors would work in their favor.

Then, of course, there was the traditional Yankee-Dodger rivalry, which went back to Brooklyn days. There had been some memorable Series between the two clubs At first it seemed as if the Dodgers were jinxed. The Yanks beat them in 1941, 1947, 1949, 1952, and 1953. Then, finally, in 1955, that great Dodger team of the '50s gave Brooklyn its first world championship, whipping the Yanks. But the next year the Bronx Bombers won again.

After the Dodgers moved to L.A. they had better luck, beating the Yanks in four straight in 1963, with Sandy Koufax winning a pair. Now, after 14 years, the two teams were pitted against each other once again.

The old rivalry was still alive. And to Steve Garvey, for one, it was very apparent.

"These are the two classic teams of the past," Steve said. "There is so much nostalgia about these clubs, and I love it. I think we're all conscious of the past and this wonderful rivalry. This is the World Series the people wanted."

The Yankees were also conscious of Steve Garvey. Their scouting report on him read, in part: "Good, smart hitter. Looks for pitcher's best pitch, especially in tight situations. He uses the entire field and will go with a pitch, especially if our pitchers pitch him one way too many times in a row."

So the Bombers knew Steve was a player to be reckoned with as the Series got under way in New York. The Dodgers opened with their pressure pitcher, Don Sutton. And the Yanks countered with a surprise, Don Gullett, who had hurt his arm in the playoffs and wasn't supposed to come back.

In the first inning it looked as if he couldn't. Davey Lopes walked and Bill Russell promptly slammed a triple to score a run. Then Reggie Smith walked and Ron Cey lofted a sacrifice fly for a second run. Gullett then picked Smith off first and after Steve drew a walk in his first Series at bat, Gullett settled down to get out of the inning. In the Yank first, singles by Munson, Jackson, and Chambliss made it a 2-1 game.

Both pitchers then took control, and the score remained the same until the bottom of the sixth when Yank second sacker Willie Randolph lined a homer to left for a 2-2 tie. In the eighth Randolph walked and Munson's hit-and-run double brought Willie home for a 3-2 Yankee lead.

But the Dodgers didn't quit. They rallied in the ninth and tied it on a two-out single by pinch hitter Lee Lacy off relief ace Sparky Lyle. The game remained stalemated until the 12th. Randolph opened the Yank half of the inning with a double off Rick Rhoden. Munson walked. Then Paul Blair, who had gone into the game in the ninth as a defensive measure, lined a single to left to win the game. The Yanks had taken a 1-0 lead in the Series.

"It came down to sudden death," said Steve, who had a bunt single in four trips, "and we ran out of time before they did."

In the second game Manager Martin gambled with Catfish Hunter, in order to give his overworked staff two more days of rest. L.A. countered with Burt Hooten. It wasn't Hunter's day. Homers by Cey, Yeager, and Smith accounted for five Dodger runs in three innings and knocked the Catfish off the mound.

Steve smashed a homer against Sparky Lyle in the ninth to put the icing on a 6-1 Dodger win. He also made a sparkling play in the field in the fourth inning. The Yanks had two on when Reggie Jackson smashed one down the line. If it got through two runs would score and a runner would be at least on second. But Steve back-handed the ball and recovered quickly to start a 3-6-3 doubleplay. One run scored, but the bases were cleared and two were out. It was one of the best defensive plays of the entire Series.

The Yanks managed just five hits off Hooten's knuckle curve ball. So L.A. came out of New York with a split and were confident as the Series headed for Los Angeles and three games there.

But in game three things started going sour for the Dodgers. Lefty Tommy John started against the Yanks' Mike Torrez. John was the hero of the play-offs, but the Yanks quickly roughed him up and tallied three in the first. Then in the Dodger third Smith and Garvey singled, and Dusty Baker clouted a three-run homer to tie the game.

An inning later the Yanks regained the lead and made it 5-3 an inning after that. Torrez, in the meantime, seemed to be getting stronger as the game went on. Garvey got another hit in the fifth, and Yeager had one in the sixth, but Torrez then retired the last eleven Dodgers in a row to nail down the win and a 2-1 Yankee lead.

In game four, young Yankee fastballer Ron Guidry fired a four-hitter at the Dodgers, beating Doug Rau and giving the Yanks a 4-2 win and a 3-1 Series lead. Reggie Jackson was the Yankee star with a double and homer, as Steve took the horsecollar in four at bats. Suddenly the Yanks were in the driver's seat. It would be Sutton and Gullett in game five.

The Dodgers didn't roll over. Instead they took out the big bats and pounded the Yankees, 10-4, getting four in the fourth, three in the fifth, and two in the sixth to put it away. Yeager and Smith had Dodger homers, while Munson and Jackson connected for the New Yorkers. Steve had two hits, including a double, as Sutton went all the way for the win, sending the Series back to the Bronx.

Before the sixth game started it was revealed that both Steve and Davey Lopes had received death threats by telephone in their hotel rooms. Neither player seemed too concerned, though that type of thing, which had happened before, must be unsettling, to say the least. Security was very tight around Yankee Stadium where the fans had been quite unruly in the past.

Game six started with Burt Hooten facing Mike Torrez. This time Hooten didn't have it, and neither did the relief pitchers. The Dodgers scored first when Steve lined a triple down the right field line to score a pair of runs. But the Yanks tied it on a two-run shot by Chris Chambliss. After that, Reggie Jackson took over.

The star outfielder, who had been the center of controversy all year long, blasted three consecutive home runs on three pitches against three different hurlers to send the Stadium crowd into a frenzy. His five RBI's helped the Yanks and Torrez nail down the series with a 8-4 victory. The Yankees were once again World Champs.

The Dodgers didn't hit well as a team for the entire

Series. But, as usual, their leading hitter was Steve Garvey. Steve banged out nine hits in 24 at bats for a .375 World Series average. The only other Dodger to hit .300 was Catcher Yeager at .316. When it was over Steve displayed his usual good sportsmanship and candor.

"When Reggie [Jackson] hit the third one I gave him a hand myself," Steve said. "After all, I've had pitchers tip their hat to me when I've hit one. You've got to appreciate a performance from time to time. I was caught up in it. Baseball is a team game, but it's a number of individual battles, and I don't think I've ever seen a performance like his in a championship situation. He beat us singlehandedly. He drove in five runs and we had four."

Jackson, when told about Steve's gesture, said it didn't surprise him.

"What a great player Steve Garvey is," Jackson said, "and what a great man. He's the best all-around human being in baseball. My one regret about not playing with the Dodgers is not being around Steve Garvey."

No one could find fault with Steve or the Dodgers. The team deserved to be in the Series and will be back. Steve, as usual, played outstanding ball in the field and at the plate. Since becoming a regular he has consistently shown himself to be a leader, a man who can be depended upon for the big hit, the big play. He knows very well that the Dodgers have quite a tradition, too, and he has had some very large shoes from the team's past to fill. But as Steve himself has often said:

"I was born to be a Dodger."

★ THURMAN MUNSON ★

★ One day, several years ago, Thurman Munson sat down, thought a minute, then put his thoughts into words for a waiting reporter.

"Well, it's this way," he said. "I'm little. I'm pudgy. I don't look good doing things. Those big, tall guys look super."

To anyone who didn't know better, this would sound like the talk of a fringe player—a guy struggling to hang on, a player lacking in confidence who feels that he's about to lose his job or that he won't be given a fair shot at a position. It sounds like a player lacking the physical equipment to be a major league ballplayer.

But the words came from a superstar, one of the best all-around catchers and hitters in the big leagues, a man who went on to win the American League's Most Valuable Player award and played on a World Series winner!

Little? At 5'-11", 190 pounds, Thurman Munson is not small.

Pudgy? Well, wasn't there a time when catchers were supposed to be built like rock-hard fireplugs? Yogi Berra didn't exactly remind people of John Wayne!

Doesn't look good doing things? In whose opinion? The fact is that he does everything well.

Those big, tall guys look super? Well, in this image-conscious world, most of us want to be something we're not.

The point is this. Thurman Munson is an All-Star; to many he is the best catcher in the American League. He plays for the New York Yankees, a team which finally regained its former glory in 1977 by winning the World Series. And Thurman Munson is the Yankee captain, the first player to hold that distinction on the club since the legendary Lou Gehrig.

From 1975 to 1977, Thurman Munson was one of the most consistent players in the major leagues. In fact, in each of those three seasons Thurman batted over .300 and drove in more than 100 runs, the first major leaguer to accomplish that since Bill White (then a Cardinal, now a Yankee broadcaster) did it in the early 1960s. No American Leaguer had done it since Ted Williams in the late 1940s.

Thurman has been a perennial All-Star and in 1976 was chosen the Most Valuable Player in the American League as he led the Yanks to their first pennant in 12 years. Yet Thurman Munson often felt neglected and unappreciated by the fans, and this bugged him.

There are several reasons for this neglect. One is Munson's basic nature. He's just not a flashy, outgoing guy. He plays hard, very hard, and is determined to win every time out. So when he loses it takes him a while to get over it, and he often appears surly and sullen to members of the press. Thus, until his MVP year in 1976, Thurman hadn't received the same amount of ink as the more outgoing players, despite some fine seasons.

Another reason is Carlton Fisk. Fisk is undoubtedly the man Munson was referring to when he said, "Those big, tall guys look super." Fisk is the catcher for the Boston Red Sox, and Thurman's main rival for the league's top receiver. He was American League Rookie of the Year in 1972, two years after Thurman had won the same distinction. Plus Fisk is tall, dark, handsome, and outgoing, and as a rookie he hit a brace of homers over Fenway Park's short leftfield wall. So to most, he was immediately the young superstar catcher of the league, the American League's answer to Johnny Bench. And Munson? Well, he just kind of became "Thurman Who?"

Munson's own annoyance started in 1973. Fisk was not having a good year. Munson was. Yet when the fans voted for the All-Star catcher, Fisk won the position by some half million votes. Munson began brooding about his popularity and his image in the eyes of the fans.

To be honest about Fisk, he is a fine ballplayer who has continued to shine for the Bosox. Which catcher is better? There's not much separating them. Perhaps it's best to say Fisk gives the Red Sox what they need most, considering Fenway and all, while Munson provides the Yanks with what they best need in spacious Yankee Stadium. Thurman does have an edge in durability. Fisk has been hurt on several occasions and has missed considerable time.

But Thurman is no longer Mr. Anonymous. There are two things guaranteed to get a good player ink— winning and controversy. The Yanks started winning in '76 with Munson the team leader and eventual league MVP. Then in '77 the team acquired free agent Reggie Jackson, along with some others, and thus began a year of almost constant dissension, with the battle lines drawn (at least by the press) between a Munson faction and a Jackson faction.

So now everyone knows about Thurman Munson. But don't get him wrong. When he talks down about himself, he's talking strictly image, not ability. He has confidence, knows what he can do, and is proud of it. So are his teammates. They once decided to kid him and told him there was a rumor that Johnny Bench was being traded to the Yanks. Without blinking an eye, Thurman said:

"Bench coming to the Yankees? Hey, that's great for us. Where's he gonna play, designated hitter?"

Munson knows he can compete with anyone behind the plate. In fact, had he played at another time, he might well have been *the* superstar at the position, and it wouldn't have mattered what kind of image he projected. Catcher used to be the position nobody wanted, but in the last decade or so, the position has been glamorized and has come into vogue. Many youngsters are now actually preparing by choice to become catchers.

There was a time when the game's great catchers could be counted on the fingertips. There were so few, and that covered maybe a half century of major league baseball. The real old timers will name the likes of Roger Bresnahan, Ray Schalk, and Gabby Street, yet they set no great records and left behind few remarkable achievements. When you mention the great players of those early days—Cobb, Wagner, Collins, Lajoie, Speaker, Jackson, Sisler, Ruth—none of them were catchers. The really good ones didn't want to go back there and take that pounding.

In the middle years of the game—the twenties, thirties, and forties—three names dominate: Gabby Hartnett, Bill Dickey, and Mickey Cochrane. These three Hall of Famers stood head and shoulders above the others and were considered the great catchers of their day and perhaps of all time. Each could handle himself behind the plate, and more importantly, each could hit. They were also great team leaders.

Then in the late forties and through the fifties, the

catching position was once again basked in anonymity. Only two names really come up when anyone is talking about the catchers of that day, and they almost always go together. They are Berra and Campanella, Yogi of the Yankees, and Campy of the Dodgers. Like Dickey, Cochrane, and Hartnett, Yogi and Campy could do it all—catch, handle pitchers, hit, hit with power, lead. Both, too, are now enshrined in the Cooperstown Hall of Fame.

But think about Berra and Campanella for a minute. Both of them were also prototypes of what a catcher should have been in those days. Both were short and stocky, powerfully built, but not exactly movie-star types. They seemed perfectly suited to squatting behind home plate and taking the pounding that goes with playing there. For a long time, most catchers seemed to resemble to some extent Berra and Campanella.

When coaches looked around they'd often pick the slowest, fattest kid to play catcher, because he could do little else and could use his bulk to "block the plate. The better athletes wanted no part of catching. They gravitated to the more glamorous positions— pitcher, short, centerfield—and took it from there.

And what did the catcher have? Well, he was immediately handed a mask; a big, cumbersome glove; a chest protector; and shin guards. Catcher's equipment. And what was this equipment called in baseball jargon? *The tools of ignorance*. The implication was clear. Anyone who was dumb enough to be a catcher deserved the tools of ignorance.

Then there were the physical risks involved in catching. It's a debilitating position. In an average nine-inning game the catcher must squat and rise an average of 200 times, a task so wearing on the legs that most catchers seem to get slower and slower as their careers progress.

And if this wasn't enough, there was always the threat of a foul tip splitting or breaking a finger, hand, or wrist. Catchers' hands were always bruised and battered, and they always played the game in some kind of pain.

Then there were the head-on collisions at home plate. The stationary catcher was always fair game for the base runner barreling in from third. How many times have you seen catchers knocked sprawling into the dust? A catcher takes the same kind of knocks that football players absorb, and if he fails to hold onto the ball, a ball park full of fans knows it immediately and shows its displeasure with boos.

There is a cute, yet apropos story involving the late, great heavyweight boxing champion, Rocky Marciano. When the Rock was a youngster he played baseball, and because of his build, he was a catcher. Finally the time came when Rocky had to choose between baseball and boxing. He chose boxing, and his mother breathed a sigh of relief. Said Mrs. Marciano: "I didn't raise my son to be a catcher!"

No wonder. Who in his right mind would want to be a catcher? And to top it off, a catcher couldn't be a dummy. He has one of the most mentally taxing jobs on the field. After all, he must be aware of the game situation, more so than anyone else. He has to know the hitters and be able to tell his pitchers how to handle them. He's got to move his infielders and outfielders around and remind them of situations that might arise. He's also got to be an amateur psychologist, drawing every ounce of strength from his pitcher, and he must know immediately when that pitcher is losing his edge. If the catcher blows it, the whole game might be lost.

Thus, for many years from the late forties to the early sixties, there wasn't much beyond Berra and Campanella. Most of the others were plodders, who were trained to handle the mitt adequately and were built to take the beating. Rarely did they contribute much with their bats. But that was an accepted part of the game then. If you had a catcher who could catch, that was blessing enough.

What changed the situation? For one thing, a young catcher with the Chicago Cubs in the mid-1960s began doing something the old-time catchers wouldn't have dreamed of doing. He was Randy Hundley, and he introduced a one-handed style of catching. Using a flexible, deep-pocketed mitt, Hundley caught his pitcher with just his gloved hand, much like a first baseman does. When the pitch was delivered, he tucked his bare hand safely behind his body, and in one quick innovation eliminated the number-one hazard of catching, the split, sprained, bruised, and broken finger, which usually occurred on that exposed hand. Imagine a kid catcher in Little League, Babe Ruth League, or high school, splitting fingers every few games. Just how long is that kid going to stay a catcher? But as soon as Hundley's style became accepted (and it didn't take long), kids everywhere were following it.

Plus there was the old business maxim of supply and demand. The lack of good catchers received more publicity as media coverage of baseball increased in the fifties and sixties, and this gave coaches and even parents the idea of encouraging youngsters to catch.

"Listen, kid. There are plenty of pitchers and outfielders. But good catchers are hard to find. Become a good catcher and you've got a better shot at making the majors."

This philosophy, too, contributed to more youngsters sticking with the position throughout their growing years. But perhaps the final cog in the catching wheel was the arrival of a dynamic young catcher on the baseball scene in 1968. He was Johnny Bench of the Cincinnati Reds.

Bench came to the majors as a poised, confident, outgoing twenty-year-old, who took over the Cincy catching job and handled it like a veteran. Almost overnight, his baseball abilities and personality gave the position a new aura of glamor. Bench seemed to be everywhere, in newspapers, magazines, on television, interviewed here and there, everywhere. And he produced. Catching with Hundley's one-handed style, he was instantly the best defensive catcher in the league. He could throw like a bullet, hit with power, and even run fairly well. And he was durable. He gave other young catchers the incentive to stay with the position instead of begging off, moving to first base or the outfield.

It didn't take long for the catchers to follow Bench and create a whole new breed behind the plate. Pittsburgh's Manny Sanguillan, who caught very well, was a top hitter, a free swinger like Clemente, but he also had the running speed of a Maury Wills. Ted Simmons of the Cards was an explosive switch hitter, another poised youngster who did it all. Munson came up about the same time, followed by Fisk, and there were other youngsters right behind who also showed great potential. Most of them could catch well, and in the age of the base stealer, also throw. Yet unlike some of their predecessors, they could also run and hit. And the young ones keep coming.

And where does this leave Thurman Munson? Undoubtedly near the top in ability, but somewhere else when it comes to charisma. Munson is just not the kind of guy who stands out in a crowd. Yet from the time he joined the Yanks in 1970, he has been marked for stardom.

Thurman Lee Munson was born on June 7, 1947, in Akron, Ohio. He grew up in nearby Canton, which is known as the home of Football's Hall of Fame. But Thurman's eye was on the Hall at Cooperstown.

It was a good childhood for Thurman, though his family didn't have much money. His father was a long-distance truck driver, so he was often away from home for days at a stretch. And as Thurman remembers:

"Truck drivers didn't make much money then, and it was really tough for him supporting a family of four kids. Yeah, we had food and clothing, all right, but not a dime left over after that."

Still, young Thurman admired his father and credits the elder Munson with giving him the attributes that later led to his success.

"My father was a go-getter," Thurm says. "I think he's the one who always made me want to play hard. He always wanted me to do better. I remember once he came to see me play in the minors. I had a great day at the plate—five for five, I think, with a couple of home runs. After the game what does my father tell me? He tells me I really looked bad behind the plate. That's the way he was. He wanted me to improve, so to my face he'd often criticize me, but to everybody else he'd say, 'Hey, that's my son.' So I always knew he was proud."

Thurm's brother Duane was also a fine athlete, but it was Thurman who had the extra incentive that led him to the majors. Thurman explains:

"Duane was a great athlete, but he didn't care that much whether he won or lost. I never could play that way. I've got to play hard. If you're that way, you don't leave yourself open to criticism. And if I don't slide hard, I can't expect the other guys to do it."

So Thurm always had the makings of a leader. As a youngster he played various sports: baseball in the summer, football in the fall, and basketball during the winter. He became an outstanding player in all three, and when he reached high school, he became a star in each.

In football, he was a wingback on offense and a linebacker on defense. The hard contact got him ready for those future collisions at the plate. And as a wingback, he had to have speed. Thurman Munson isn't slow.

He wasn't slow on the basketball court, either. He couldn't be, because he played guard and averaged some twenty points per game. He was good enough on the hardwood to be selected for the All-County team his senior year.

That left baseball. There was never any doubt that baseball was Thurm's best sport, yet prior to his senior year in high school, he wasn't a catcher. He shied away from the position for the same reasons so many other youngsters did. He preferred to play shortstop, and he played both short and second base during his first two years. Then in his senior year, when the need arose, team-player Munson volunteered to move behind the plate.

He took to the position very quickly, surprising his coaches and teammates alike. And he enjoyed playing there, because he was really in the game and could lead from his backstop slot. The physical part didn't bother him, and once he mastered some of the other fundamentals, he was outstanding.

Despite his obvious baseball ability, Thurm found himself flooded with scholarship offers to play college football. Football, of course, is a much more glamorous college sport than baseball, and there are many more recruiters shopping around with offers. Thurm was flattered, yet hesitant.

"I knew baseball was my best sport, and I wanted to continue at it. Even if I played college football and did well, I knew I'd never play in the pros. But I needed a scholarship to attend college, and I kept waiting."

Finally, the one he wanted came along. Kent State University in Ohio offered him a baseball scholarship and he grabbed it. By then he was committed to catching, and he immediately became an outstanding player at Kent State. He was also thinking of the major leagues by then. So he worked extra hard to attract attention. After all, Kent State wasn't exactly at the zenith of the college baseball world. The school isn't usually spoken of in the same breath as, say, Arizona State, or USC. But they played a good schedule and the scouts came.

Yet even then Thurm wasn't the flashy type. He often went unnoticed, as he did the little things that help win ball games. The fact that he still wasn't an outstanding hitter didn't help. He was good enough to become an All-America choice after the 1968 season, but it was his last year and he began to worry. What he didn't know at the time was that there was a scout watching him, watching him very closely.

The man was Gene Woodling, a name that should sound familiar to baseball fans. Woodling was a star outfielder with the New York Yankees in the late forties and fifties, when the Yanks were reeling off world championships like they were duck soup. An outstanding hitter, Woodling contributed mightily to many a Yankee victory. Now he was a chief scout for the Yanks, an important job because the scouts are the men who keep the talent rolling in.

There was a time when scouts had even more power. Clubs entrusted these wily judges of talent to sign players right on the spot. The classic story is that of veteran scout Tom Greenwade signing Mickey Mantle to a Yankee contract before anyone in the Yankee organization even laid eyes on him.

"It's not at all that way today," Gene Woodling says. "Today we have the free-agent draft, where teams choose players in order, much as they do in football and basketball. And the team that picks the player is the only one that can bid for his services. If they can't reach an agreement, then the player goes back into the pool and can be drafted again.

"It's a good system in that it eliminates much of the backbiting and lying that went on. A scout can't make a boy false promises because the parent club controls the draft. And this way, all the scouts help each other and kind of work together. There's no way you can hide a good boy, so you might as well let the other guy know about him. He might help you by showing you a boy that would better suit your club's needs."

Gene Woodling knew that the Yankees needed a catcher in 1968. In fact, it was the first time in many years that the club did not have a first-rate backstop, which had been as much of a Yankee tradition as anything else.

The great Bill Dickey caught for the Bronx Bombers from 1928 to 1946, getting nearly 2,000 hits and compiling a life-time average of .313. Many consider him the greatest catcher of all time. Dickey retired as an active player in 1946, the same year that a youngster named Larry "Yogi" Berra came to the Yanks.

Yogi took over the number one job and held it right into the 1960s. Another Hall of Famer, Yogi blasted 358 home runs and was named the American League's Most Valuable Player three times. He is remembered as a fine catcher and one of the most dangerous clutch hitters of all time.

When Yogi retired in 1963, the Yanks already had his successor; in fact, Elston Howard had been splitting the job with Yogi for a number of seasons. Howard came to the majors later in baseball life than most, and didn't have as long a career as the other two. But he took over from Yogi and held the job until 1967. He, too, was an outstanding catcher and strong hitter, and he also took the American League's MVP prize one year.

So from 1928 until 1967, a period of forty years, the New York Yankees always had one of baseball's best catchers receiving for them. But there was no immediate replacement when Howard left, and several players shared the position for the next few seasons. That's why all the Yankee scouts were keeping especially alert for any bright young catching prospects. And Gene Woodling found one at Kent State in 1968.

What does a scout look for in a player? Gene talked about that and about which of those qualities he saw in young Thurman Munson:

"First of all, we have to look at a lot of ballplayers, so we've got to be able to evaluate a boy quickly. My territory, for instance, consists of all of Ohio and Michigan, and parts of Kentucky and Indiana. I have two other men working for me and the three of us have to cover everything in these states. When you think that there are some sixty-eight colleges playing baseball in Ohio alone, you begin to get the total picture. We not only cover colleges, but also high schools, Legion games and any other leads that might come in. It's a mammoth job."

The first thing Gene Woodling looks at when he's scouting a youngster is the boy's speed and his arm:

"These two things are a must for a major leaguer.

No way a guy is going to make it if he has minimal throwing skills and little speed. Some guys also look at size. I don't. A kid of 5'-8" or 5'-9" can certainly play big league ball.

"So what I'm looking for are basic tools. I know you're probably wondering why I didn't mention hitting. I have a reason. There's just no way you can figure out that bat. I played major league ball for almost twenty years, and I never figured it out. A kid can hit a ton in high school or college, then he runs into curves, sliders, the whole bit, and comes up empty."

What was Gene's first reaction when he saw Thurman Munson at Kent State?

"The first thing I noticed about Thurman was his speed," recalls Gene. "He was exceptionally fast for a catcher. As you know, catchers can sometimes get away with being rather slow, but this kid could run.

"Then I noticed his arm. It was strong, not the strongest I'd ever seen, but strong enough. The thing about it was the quickness. Thurm had, and still has, the quickest arm I've ever seen on a catcher, and I think he's proved it in the big leagues. Anyway, when I saw him throw I was just about convinced."

So those were the basics that Gene Woodling looked for. He liked what he saw that first time, then tried to see a bit more when he returned, for he already had Munson high on his list of possibilities:

"As I watched him some more, I could see that he already had outstanding ability as a catcher. In other words, defensively, he was major league caliber. He stood out like a light bulb with those guys he was playing with.

"His hitting was just so-so. In fact, I had some reservations about it, but as I said, that's the last thing I worry about. In fact, I'll admit now that Thurm's hit a lot better than I thought he would since he's been in the majors. Anyway, it didn't take long for me to decide he was the real goods."

Unlike some scouts, Gene didn't rush up to Munson, introduce himself, and try to sell the youngster a bill of goods. Instead he simply submitted Thurm's name to the Yankee office with his recommendation and let them take it from there.

"There were a large number of scouts around Thurman that year," Gene remembers, "yet I never met him in person. I'd rather not let a boy know I'm there watching him. That way, he'll just play naturally. Once the Yanks picked Thurman, I went back in, introduced myself, and did the actual signing."

Perhaps because of his childhood, Thurman was highly motivated by money. Oh, sure, he had a driving desire to excel and win, but he also wanted to be compensated for it. He signed with the Yanks for a modest bonus, as much as he thought he was worth then, and immediately went about the business of making the big leagues—but not before he began juggling his money.

"I was always interested in money," Thurm admitted. "But when I first signed, got my bonus, and saw how much tax they took out of it, I said, 'My God, if they're gonna do this to me—if I ever really start making some money, I'm gonna be in trouble. So I took the little money I had left after taxes and put it into real estate."

Thurm's salary has, of course, moved into the upper brackets, but he still invests carefully, hoping to lay the groundwork for a going business when he retires.

But back to baseball. After signing Munson, the Yanks immediately sent him to Binghamton, New York, where he played in seventy-one games before the 1968 season ended. But he was impressive, catching very well and hitting .301, with 68 hits in 226 at bats. He had six homers and 37 RBI's. At age twenty-one, he seemed to be progressing rapidly. That was good news, because the Yanks needed him.

By now, everyone knows the story of the New York Yankees, and how they dominated the game of baseball for nearly four and one-half decades, from the early 1920s to the mid-1960s. Between 1921 and 1964, the Yankees won 29 American League pennants and 20 world championships, a record miles ahead of any other team.

From 1949 to 1964, the club took 14 pennants in 16 years, an amazing achievement, winning 5 in a row twice and 4 straight once. And the first 5, from 1949 to 1953, resulted in 5 consecutive world titles. They were the supreme dynasty in all of sports.

But after the 1964 season the team suddenly fell apart. Veteran stars like Mantle, Maris, Ford, Pepitone, Boyer, and Tresh all seemed to go at once—some to age, some prematurely. But they stopped producing at the same time and in the space of a single season the club nosedived from first to sixth. A year later, in 1966, they fell to tenth and were last in the American League. They were ninth the year after that, then seemed to level off and play around the .500 mark in 1968 and 1969. But it wasn't the same.

In 1969, Thurman was sent to Syracuse, the Yanks' top farm team in the International League. He played just twenty-eight games there, starring with a .363 batting average and catching extremely well. Then the Yanks called him to the Bronx and the big club. He had played just ninety-nine games in the minors, and he was never to return. When someone asked Thurm why he worked so hard to get to the majors he gave a typical answer:

"You don't get rich playing in Syracuse."

But it was also pride and desire. Thurm felt he was ready, and he was happy to get the call. He spent the remainder of the 1969 season as a backup for veteran Jake Gibbs. Though he played in just twenty-six games, he did well, batting .256 on 22 for 86, hitting his first homer, and driving in nine runs. His poise and ability behind the plate surprised everyone as well.

So when spring training for 1970 rolled around, the Yanks decided to give Thurman a real shot at the starting job. The veteran Gibbs was still there, but they knew what he could do. Another youngster, John Ellis, was also in the sweepstakes.

As the exhibition season unfolded, both Munson and Ellis were hitting a ton; both were well over .300 and looked extremely good. The difference was that Thurman was a much more accomplished catcher at that time. Ellis, though big and strong, did not have Thurm's skills behind the plate. So toward the end of the practice games, Ellis was moved to first base. Both rookies had won jobs and the Yanks were excited about the upcoming season.

Before opening day, Thurm was talking about his chances for a strong rookie year, and he was already mentioning the fact that he didn't have classic form:

"I don't see why I shouldn't have a good year. I've been preparing for this for a long time, working hard toward it, and I feel I'm ready. I know there are people who don't agree with me. I remember when I was at Kent State and the scouts were beginning to come. There was one guy, from the Cleveland Indians, who said I couldn't run, said I couldn't play in the big leagues. I don't know who he was looking at because I could run in high school. I was fast. But that's just what I mean about not looking good when I do things."

So the Yanks opened the 1970 season with some

new faces in the lineup. Yet in a matter of weeks, the new faces seemed destined to disappear. Both Thurm and Ellis, the hottest hitters in the spring, were suddenly cool when the real thing started. Each was struggling, and fans began to wonder if they were just spring phenoms, the kind that cause all sorts of excitement, then fizzle out just as quickly, never to be seen again.

For awhile it seemed as if Thurman Munson might fit into that category. After his first 30 at bats of 1970, Thurm had just one hit! One hit in 30 at bats! That's a batting average of .033. Reporters were already beginning to stay away from the youngster, figuring he'd have nothing to say, and also figuring he wouldn't be around much longer. But one brave soul ventured up to Thurm and asked him if he thought he could pull his game together. The answer he got was surprising.

"Don't worry about me," Thurm said. "When this year is over I'll be hitting .300."

The reporter couldn't believe it. Neither could anyone else. Here was this raw rookie, off to a horrendous start at the plate, still having the gumption to predict a .300 season. Some people laughed, the serious ones tried to show how difficult it would be for a player to pick up the slack from a start like that.

"He could get 25 hits in his next 70 at bats," said one, "and that's a .357 clip in itself. Yet it would just give him a .260 mark for his first 100 at bats of the season. It's a long way to come."

The thing that kept Thurman in the lineup was his glove, his ability to handle the pitchers and the game behind the plate. He caught with the poise of a veteran, and he made even the older pitchers feel comfortable working to him.

"He gives you a lot of confidence out there," said

one veteran. "You start pitching to him, and you forget he's just twenty-three years old."

Another said, "I remember reading stories about Bench, how he bawled out veteran pitchers his first year. This kid is the same way. If he feels you're not putting out, or not doing something right, he lets you know about it in no uncertain terms. He's not afraid to speak out."

It was just a question of how long the Yanks could put up with Munson's anemic bat. They were already beginning to platoon Ellis at first. His start had been almost as horrible as Thurm's. Could the benching of Munson be far behind?

It's doubtful that the Yanks would have waited much longer. But they didn't have to. Thurman finally began to hit. And he began to hit well. From that point on, he was to hold up both ends of his job.

As the year wore on, it became obvious that Thurman's hitting was solid and steady. No more bad slumps. And the Yanks were having a good year. They were trailing powerful Baltimore but were playing well over .500 ball and showing signs of revival. They never did catch the Orioles, but they finished the year with a 93-69 mark, good for second place in the Eastern Division of the American League.

And Thurman Munson had given the Yanks even more than they hoped for. Amazingly, he had made good his promise, hitting .302 (a club-leading figure) for the season and .312 after that disastrous start. He played in 132 games and got 137 hits, including 6 homers and 53 RBI's. He was also outstanding behind the plate, working well with his pitchers and exhibiting that quick throwing arm that Gene Woodling had talked about. Base runners didn't take too many liberties with Thurman Munson back there.

It wasn't until several weeks after the season ended

that Thurm really got the good news. He had been named American League Rookie of the Year for 1970.

But the next season, both Thurm and the Yankees fell back. The team barely played .500 ball, while Munson, off to another excruciatingly slow start, didn't recover quite as rapidly, finishing at just .251 with 10 homers and 42 RBI's in 125 games.

The only plus was his catching. There was little doubt now that he was one of the best receivers in baseball. It was his catching skills that got him selected to the All-Star team for the first time, and when the year ended he had some noteworthy catching stats.

Thurman led all major league receivers, including Bench, with a .998 fielding mark. He had committed just a single error in 615 chances, tying a Yankee catching mark held by Elston Howard. He had also thrown out 23 of the 38 runners who tried to steal on him. And far fewer were running on him than in his rookie season when they were all anxious to test him. There didn't seem to be any way to stop him from becoming the next catching star in the American League.

Then in 1972, another young catcher burst upon the A.L. He was Carlton Fisk of the Boston Red Sox, and without any advance notice, he began to take the league by storm. Playing in ancient Fenway Park with its short left-field wall, Fisk took advantage of the "Green Monster" and began hitting shots over it. Not that he didn't have power. Fisk was big and strong, a striking figure on the field, and this helped him attract new legions of fans. Ironically, his nickname was "Pudge," a name tagged on him years earlier, when he was heavier. Now, however, he symbolized to Thurman Munson, the typical long, lean, good-looking athlete. Munson thought of himself more as "pudge."

It wasn't that Fisk was having a better year than Munson. He wasn't, though he was producing more runs via the homer and RBI route. But the Yanks were faltering while the Sox were in a pennant race. And in August, Fisk's name hit the baseball world when, as a rookie, he publicly criticized such veterans Carl Yastrzemski and Reggie Smith for not hustling.

All kinds of stories hit the wires on the young catcher, and his picture made the cover of national sports magazines, with titles such as "The Rookie Who Roused the Red Sox." Some writer mentioned that the handsome Fisk looked a lot like movie star Charlton Heston. And so forth. So by the time the 1972 season ended, it was Carlton Fisk, not Thurman Munson, who was the American League's answer to Johnny Bench. And a rivalry was born between the two that continues to this day.

There wasn't a whole lot to choose from in the stats. Thurman had a good year, both at the plate and in the field. He upped his average to .280, hitting 7 homers and drove home 46 runs; while Fisk hit .293, with 22 homers and 61 RBI's. Fisk's bat had certainly been more productive, but Thurman had been a .300 hitter as a rookie. Then, like Munson before him, Fisk was named American League Rookie of the Year.

Thurm's image troubles really started during 1973. He was having a good year at the plate, his best ever, since his power production was up and his batting average around the .300 mark. Fisk, in the meantime, was still hitting homers over the wall in Boston, but his average was hovering around the .250 mark. And while Fisk was good defensively, there really weren't too many people who would claim he was better than Munson. Yet Fisk was more of a holler guy, more vocal, and thus his name was always in the papers. As they say in the press, he was "good copy."

That's undoubtedly part of the reason that Fisk beat out Munson for the starting berth on the All-Star team. But when he beat him out by some half million votes, Munson really fumed; he couldn't keep quiet about it any longer.

Finally, he popped off to a reporter. "I'm not taking anything away from Fisk," said Munson, "but get him away from Fenway Park and that easy wall in left field and see how many home runs he hits."

Not one to take those matters lightly, Fisk responded to the challenge:

"I don't want to bad-mouth Munson," said Carlton, "but he is jealous of me. He wants to be the American League All-Star catcher, but I took it away from him. He always wants to talk when he comes to bat. He must think he's another Yogi Berra, which he isn't."

Bang! Just like that there was a feud. And when there's a hint of a feud in the air reporters come around. Suddenly, more of them than ever wanted to talk with Thurman Munson, and before long the discussion would come down to a matter of Fisk and recognition.

"Everybody wants recognition," Thurm said. "And the best way to get recognition is to hit forty home runs or win twenty games as a pitcher. I'm a line drive hitter, so the best way for me to get recognition is to have the Yankees get into the World Series."

But Thurm admitted that he felt image also had something to do with it, and in that respect, he wasn't the perfect example of the classic catcher.

"I don't throw the ball as hard as some catchers," he said, "but I get it where I want it to go. I'm squatty, I have a big hind end, and I say what I think. But I'll tell you something. I bet if you ask Ralph [Yankee manager Ralph Houk] if he'd trade me one-on-one with anyone, there'd be only one person he'd do it for, and that would be Johnny Bench."

The All-Star Game came and went, with Munson serving as backup for starter Fisk. But the harsh words of the earlier time weren't forgotten. And on August 1, 1973, the whole thing boiled over.

The Yanks were playing the Red Sox up at Fenway. Both were still in the pennant race and it was a hard-fought game, as most Yankee-Red Sox games are. It was tied at 2-2 in the ninth inning; Yanks up.

Munson was batting against Red Sox lefthander John Curtis, and he promptly rapped a hard double to left. When Graig Nettles grounded out, Munson ran to third. Now Felipe Alou was up. He was walked intentionally, bringing up short-stop Gene Michael. That's when Manager Houk called for a suicide squeeze.

The suicide squeeze is one of baseball's most exciting plays. As the pitcher winds up, the runner on third breaks for home. It's then up to the batter to bunt the ball—almost anywhere—because if he gets his bat on it, the breaking runner will almost always make it. But if he misses, then there's a play at the plate with the odds against the runner. It's exciting because the play is committed from the time the runner breaks. Even if the pitch is in the dirt, the batter must go after it, because the runner has usually passed the point of no return.

So Munson was coming hard. Curtis threw a low outside curve that Michael had to lunge for. He missed. Thurm could have stopped, but instead he kept on running. He barreled into Fisk full force and the two went rolling on the ground. Thurman got up swinging. Without hesitating, Fisk swung back.

When Fisk's fist grazed Michael, who was still in the box, he jumped into the fray. Players from both dugouts rushed onto the field as Munson and Fisk were still trying to get at each other. Finally a couple of Red Sox got Munson and pinned him to the ground, thus ending the brawl.

But it didn't end for Thurm. He was still angry when reporters asked him about the incident several days later.

"I weigh 190 pounds," he said. "I'm no Lou Brock. What good would it have done me to get caught in a rundown. So I ran over Fisk. I just felt that he kicked me off him when I did it. He said the next day, in the papers, that the reason he kicked me off was so that he could get up and throw. Well, fine. But at the time, that explanation didn't satisfy me. So I got up and hit him."

There's generally no winner and loser in baseball fights. They end up as hapless wrestling matches with a lot of guys pushing and shoving. But witnesses say Fisk had a cut under his right eye and one on the chin. Munson was unmarked, and even managed to see something positive in the whole thing.

"For me, the hassle with Fisk turned into a lot of national press," he said. "Even being notorious is better than being ignored."

In a way, Thurm was right. The brawl with Fisk got him more press than usual and brought to light their rivalry for American League catching supremacy. As a consequence, more people than ever watched the two during the second half of the 1973 season. And the turn of events in that last few months of the year must have pleased Thurm very much.

He continued to wield a hot bat, while Fisk faltered. In fact, many fans began to look at Thurm in a different light. He was seen as a kind of leader of the Yanks, a silent leader who let his deeds on the diamond, not his mouth, do the talking for him.

He was also being looked upon more and more as the good guy in the Boston brawl, not so much because of anything he did, but because Carlton Fisk seemed to be in another melee each week. First there was a home plate brawl with Al Gallagher of the Angels. Then another Angel, Bob Oliver, had to be restrained from going after Fisk by five teammates. In addition, Fisk almost came to blows with veteran outfield great Frank Robinson. There were quotes floating around the league that Fisk was becoming too big for his britches.

Thurm was probably more contented with himself than ever before in the final months of the 1973 season. He sensed a measure of vindication for the All-Star snub, and he knew he was completing his finest season. The one problem was that the Yanks had again dropped out of the pennant race. The team wasn't strong enough to make a real run at it.

At the end, Thurm had hit .301, with 20 home runs and 74 RBI's (both career highs for him). He had 156 hits in 519 at bats. Fisk, by contrast, had just 125 hits in 508 at bats. He hit more homers than Thurm, getting 26, but drove in just 71 runs and batted .246. The edge had to go to Munson.

While Thurman Munson still wasn't a household name across America, the respect for the solid catcher was enormous among members of the Yankee family. Before the 1974 season started, ex-ballplayer turned Yankee sportscaster, Bill White, talked about Munson and his talents.

"Bench is the only catcher in either league who might be better than Munson right now," said Bill. "Anybody like Thurm, who uses the whole field to hit is a good hitter. Look at the guys who consistently hit .300—Aaron, Rose, Carew—they hit the ball all over. Munson does that. He can hit the ball to right field, he can hit and run for you."

New Yankee manager Bill Virdon, who took over for Ralph Houk during the 1973 season, loved the catcher he inherited with the job.

"If I had twenty-five guys like Thurman Munson, I wouldn't even have to manage this team," said Virdon. "He does everything well. He's aggressive. He's not as big as some good ones I've seen, but he's strong and quick. There's also a lot of enthusiasm in him. His only defect may be that sometimes he throws a little too enthusiastically."

Bill White agreed with that:

"Sometimes it seems that Thurm wants to gun that guy down at second by fifteen yards instead of getting him by three or four feet. When that happens, he ends up throwing the ball into centerfield. But as for the strength of his arm, let's face it, to be a catcher you don't have to have that much of a gun. Thurm is quick. I've been in baseball a long time, and I have yet to see anybody outrun a baseball."

Rushing some throws was just an outgrowth of Thurm's overall desire and enthusiasm. He's always played hard. It was just a matter of getting his game under a bit more control.

When 1974 started it looked like a promising year for both Thurm and the Yanks. The team was hanging close to the American League lead, and Munson was off to a pretty good start, which for him, a notoriously slow starter, was a blessing. In addition, Munson's rival, Fisk, was on the shelf with a serious knee injury that required surgery. Munson would have the field to himself.

Then it happened. It was still early in the season when a left-handed batter took a big riff at the ball and missed. His backswing came way back and caught

Munson on his right hand. It was a painful injury and Thurm was taken to the hospital for X-rays. Fortunately, they were negative—no broken bones, just a very bad bruise. The hand really pained Thurm, but the Yanks were finally in a pennant race and he didn't want to stay out of the lineup. So he begged in, and Manager Virdon gave him the green light. With a pennant race on and no broken bones in the hand, no way Thurm was going to stay out of that lineup a day longer than was absolutely necessary.

But he should have. Getting back in there too soon caused other problems, both in the field and at the bat. Since his hand still hadn't healed properly, Munson was forced to grip both ball and bat differently. He couldn't swing well either, and his average dropped off. Behind the plate the altered grip didn't make for good throwing, so Thurm tried to compensate. He began throwing another way and came up with elbow problems. And the hand couldn't complete the healing process because it was always being aggravated by catching or swinging the bat. The injury lingered, and it affected Thurm's play.

Yet he hung in there, right to the end, as the Yanks stayed in the pennant race right up until the final weekend of the season, losing out by a mere two games. Thurm's stats weren't bad, but in view of the '73 season, he felt they were disappointing. He finished with a .261 average, 13 homers, and 60 RBI's.

"I definitely would have had the better numbers if it wasn't for the hand. I'm not trying to make excuses, but I really couldn't grip the bat properly and my whole defensive game was hurting. It's disappointing to me because I felt I could have helped the club a lot more. Maybe if I didn't hurt the hand we would have come out on top."

As usual, Thurm was thinking of the team first. But

he Yanks had done well, especially since they hadn't
even been in their home park. The legendary Yankee
Stadium was being renovated, modernized so it could
compete with the newer parks in the league. The
Yanks played all their home games in 1974 at Shea
Stadium, the home of the National League Mets.
They'd be playing at Shea again in 1975, before re-
turning to their own park in 1976.

And by now the Yankee brass was getting pennant
hungry. The team hadn't won since 1964, by far the
longest winless stretch since that first flag in 1921. So
during the off-season they began to make some big
moves.

First of all, there was a major trade with the San
Francisco Giants. The Yanks gave up their big star,
Bobby Murcer, who was supposed to be the next Di-
Maggio or Mantle. But Bobby, a good ballplayer, always played in the shadows of those two greats. He
wasn't the power hitter they were, though he often
tried to be. And when he was moved from centerfield
to right, to make room for the slick fielding Elliott
Maddox, he began to sulk. A change had to be made.

In return for Murcer, the Yanks got Bobby Bonds,
one of the most exciting players in the major leagues.
The speedy Bonds was a powerhouse, a player who
could do it all, having a career high of 39 homers. He
was also capable of stealing more than 50 bases a year
and often batted leadoff for the Giants. But Bonds,
too, played in a shadow. He was always expected to
be the next Willie Mays, and those shoes are too big
for any man to fill. So the trade was looked upon as
beneficial to both teams.

Then the Yanks really pulled a coup. The Oakland
A's superpitcher, Jim "Catfish" Hunter, won a court
battle against team owner Charles O. Finley and was
declared a free agent. Teams in both leagues bid for

Catfish's services, and the Yankees won, with something like a $3.75 million offer for five years.

With Bonds and Hunter added to a roster that already included Thurm Munson, Roy White, Elliott Maddox, Graig Nettles, Lou Pinella, Ron Blomberg, and others, the Yanks were suddenly favorites to take the A.L. flag. The pressure was on.

The Yanks got off the mark fairly well, keeping within striking distance of the top. But it wasn't Hunter or Bonds who led the early-season surge. It was Munson, who was off to the best start of his career. The hand seemed well again, and Thurm was hitting well over .300. Manager Virdon installed him in the fourth spot in the order, the clean-up spot, and he continued to do the job.

In his own way, he was also becoming the team leader. In fact, word began drifting out of the Yankee organization that Munson was now "the soul of the team," that he was "the one player the Yankees could least afford to lose." Thurm was valuable, all right.

The story also came out that Munson was instrumental in the Yankees' signing of Hunter, that he called Catfish several times during the negotiation period to persuade him to accept the Yank's offer.

And it was Thurman Munson who became Bobby Bonds' biggest booster when Bonds was in an early-season slump. Thurman constantly worked at settling Bobby down, trying to ease the pressure and reminding him that "we all know you can hit." And slowly, Bonds began coming out of it. In fact, he went on a tear and jumped to the top of the league in homers and RBI's. And by the end of May, the Yanks had also jumped to the top of their division.

Naturally, it was Bonds and the fast-recovering Hunter who were getting the publicity. There was also much talk about the contributions of Roy White and

Elliott Maddox, both of whom went on early-season batting tears. Then Graig Nettles took off on one of his patented hitting sprees. Once again, not much notice came to Munson, who was still way over .300 and playing steady ball. It bugged him again. One writer called him the "tormented all-star." And he still chafed when someone mentioned Carlton Fisk. Oddly enough, Fisk, who had missed almost all of 1974 with a knee injury, was on the disabled list again, this time with a broken arm. But it didn't stop Thurm from sounding off when someone mentioned Fisk.

"Compared to him, why should I be so over-looked," he said. "He's a good ballplayer, but I don't think he's much of a threat in other parks as he is in Boston; he might be a better ballplayer than I am, but he has never done the things I've done—set a defensive record for catchers, set a record for assists, hit .300 twice. And in six and a half years in the big leagues, how many games have I missed?

"I know I run better than him, and I know nobody plays harder than I do. Now Johnny Bench is different. I've never hit 40 home runs or driven in 120 runs. I haven't done those things. So I can't talk about me being as good as Bench because I haven't done what he's done.

"Sometimes I wonder why playing hard hasn't helped my image. But it hasn't. Pete Rose plays that way. Charlie Hustle they call him. He gets more recognition for hustling than he does for playing the game, and he's a great player. I've always played hard. I thought that's the way you were supposed to play."

It might have sounded like sour grapes to some, but Munson was just being honest, saying the things that were on his mind. Maybe he's harped on the recognition bit for a long time, but when a player is as good as Thurm, he has the right.

Anyway, the Yankees were going real well into June when disaster struck. First Maddox went out with a knee injury that finished him for the year. One of the best defensive outfielders in the business and a .300 hitter, he had been the glue that held the outfield together. And shortly after that, Bonds hurt a knee. The injury was not bad enough to keep Bonds out, but like Munson's hand injury of the year before, it hampered his performance for the rest of the season.

After that it seemed like a jinx. Hard-hitting Ron Blomberg threw his shoulder out and kissed the season goodbye. Outfielder Lou Pinella suffered a mysterious inner ear problem that required corrective surgery. Pitchers Doc Medich, Pat Dobson, and Sparky Lyle all performed at levels below their best. In effect, a good portion of the team was either hurt or slumping. The team suddenly dropped right out of the race.

Almost everyone was affected by the team slump—except Thurman Munson. He was playing his heart out, staying up among the league leaders in hitting and RBI's. He was the starting All-Star catcher by a large margin (Fisk was still injured), and people began saying he had a good shot at the league's MVP prize.

Thurm's pace never slowed, but the Yankees never picked up. Near the end of the year Manager Virdon was fired, and he was replaced by the volatile Billy Martin, an ex-Yankee, whose thoughts immediately turned to next year. And in August, team president Gabe Paul admitted the season had been very disappointing to him.

"There have been ups and downs in my baseball life," Paul said, "but this year has been very frustrating for us. We all expected better. The whole country expected better."

So the season was a real downer. And it was a shame, since Thurman Munson had the greatest season of his career. He came to bat 597 times, collecting 190 hits for a .318 average, third best in the league. Though he hit just 12 homers, he nevertheless became the first Yankee since 1964 to drive in more than 100 runs, finishing with 102. Had the Yankees been in the pennant race, or won it, most experts feel that Thurm would have indeed been the league's MVP. He was certainly the most valuable member of the Yankees.

"My hand didn't hurt at all this year," said Thurm, "but it still wasn't as strong as I would have liked. I think I could have hit more home runs if it had been stronger. I wasn't getting that extra ten feet that can mean the difference between a homer and a drive to the wall."

Ironically, when his greatest season ended, Thurm Munson found himself still haunted by the specter of Carlton Fisk. Fisk returned to the Red Sox lineup in the second half of the season and played brilliantly. Though he didn't qualify for the batting race, he hit .331, with 10 homers and 52 RBI's in an abbreviated season. And he helped his team win the American League pennant. Fisk was then a central figure in the World Series, hitting a pair of homers, one of which (coming in extra innings) tied the series in game six. Experts call that game one of the greatest ever played.

Even though the Cincinnati Reds won the Series in seven games, the Sox came out of it as something akin to folk heroes. And because of his personal heroics, Fisk re-established himself in the minds of many as the best catcher in the American League. The chances were it would stay that way unless the Yankees could get back on top.

In 1976, the team would be returning to a refurbished Yankee Stadium. A championship would be a great way to celebrate, and owner George Steinbrenner was intent on doing just that, no matter how much money it cost.

The shape of the team was changing. Billy Martin would be the manager from day one, and new players were coming in. Three new starting pitchers were added: righthanders Dock Ellis and Ed Figueroa, and lefty Ken Holtzman. Departing were Doc Medich and Pat Dobson. In a trade with the California Angels, the Yanks added fleet centerfielder Mickey Rivers and gave up Bobby Bonds. Rivers would be needed since Elliott Maddox had undergone a second operation on his knee.

Lefty hitters Oscar Gamble and Carlos May also came over, with the club hoping they'd pick up the slack left by another injury to Ron Blomberg. And in a trade with the Pirates, the Yanks picked up a rookie second-baseman ticketed for instant stardom. His name was Willie Randolph. So there were a whole group of new players joining the club, and hopes were high.

Of course, there were still the Red Sox. The old arch-rivals figured to be the two best teams in the American League East. And in an indirect kind of way, that would set up a confrontation between Munson and Fisk once again.

In a sense it never happened, and the reason was that the Red Sox did an el foldo. They just didn't play up to their 1975 level and were never really in the race. Surprisingly enough, it was the rebuilding Baltimore Orioles who gave chase for part of the year. But during the second half it was all Yankees, and they were able to coast home with a 97-62 record, winning their division by an easy 10½ games.

Several of the Yanks had a fine year. Rivers hit .312 and stole 43 bases. Graig Nettles was brilliant at third and led the league in home runs with 32, also driving in 93 runs. Chris Chambliss had a .293 mark with 96 RBI's. Roy White was a steady .286 with 31 steals, and rookie Randolph played fine ball, hitting .267 with 37 steals. The Yanks had become something of a running team.

Figueroa led the pitchers with 19 wins, followed by Catfish and Ellis with 17 each. Sparky Lyle was the bullpen ace once more with 23 saves, and big Dick Tidrow had 10. But the main man throughout the season was Thurman Munson.

Despite a broken right index finger in spring training, Thurm recovered and was the Yanks DH on opening day. And by the time they opened at home a week later he was back behind the plate. You just couldn't keep him out of the lineup.

He was the club leader, all right, and also its best clutch hitter. Time and again he was the catalyst in a late-inning rally, and on 17 occasions his hit provided the game-winner, best on the club.

When the season ended he had a .302 batting average, 17 home runs and 105 runs batted in. He struck out only 37 times in 616 at bats, and also managed to steal a career high 14 bases. It was a great all-around season for him and many people were mentioning him as a strong MVP candidate.

"Baseball only means one thing to me," Thurm said, when asked about the possibility of getting the MVP. "That's winning. I have just one more accomplishment this year, to get into the World Series. And I plan to do it!"

Getting into the World Series meant beating the Kansas City Royals in a best of five playoff series. That wouldn't be easy. The Royals had a young, hungry team. Originally an expansion club, they were flexing their muscles for the first time and wanted to go all the way.

The playoff was bitterly fought the whole way. The two teams seemed to be starting a new rivalry, and there was no love lost between them. The series opened in Kansas City, but that didn't deter Catfish Hunter and the Yanks. They won easily, 4-1, to get off to a 1-0 lead. But the Royals came back to win the next, 7-3.

In game three the Yanks used a strong effort by Dock Ellis to win, 5-3, but K.C. tied it again in the fourth, 7-4, this time knocking out Hunter early. So the fifth and deciding game had K.C. ace Dennis Leonard going against Ed Figueroa.

Both teams scored a pair of runs in the first. The Royals got another in the second, but the Yanks got two in the third and two in the sixth to make it a 6-3 game. Then in the eighth the Royals scored three runs to tie it. That's how it stood going into the last of the ninth, Chris Chambliss leading off against fireballing reliever Mark Littell.

Littell's first pitch was a fastball down the middle and Chambliss jumped on it. As the ball soared into the right centerfield bleachers the Yanks and the fans at the Stadium went wild. Chambliss couldn't even make it around the bases. The Yankees had their first American League flag since 1964.

Many of the Yanks played well against K.C., but none better than Thurman Munson, who had 10 hits in 23 at bats for a five-game average of .435. Still, Thurm and the rest of the team would need to get up again, because in the World Series they'd be meeting the defending World Champion Cincinnati Reds, a devastating team with the likes of Johnny Bench, Joe Morgan, Tony Perez, George Foster, Ken Griffey,

Dave Concepcion, Cesar Geronimo, and one Pete Rose. The only weak suit was the starting pitchers, but Cincy had a strong bullpen. They'd be tough to beat.

Perhaps the Yanks didn't realize how tough. In the first game the Reds started their ace lefty, Don Gullett, against Doyle Alexander, who happened to be the Yanks most rested pitcher. Alexander did well, but the Reds chipped away and won it, 5-1, as Gullett and Pedro Borbon combined for a five-hitter. Borbon came on in the eighth when Gullett hurt an ankle. The Reds didn't know it then, but they wouldn't miss him at all.

Game two was a tight one, Catfish Hunter battling Fred Norman. Catfish stayed in right to the end, but the Redlegs scored in the last of the ninth to break a three-all tie and win it, 4-3. They now took a two-game lead back to New York.

Being at the Stadium with its cheering throngs didn't help the Yanks. This time rookie Pat Zachry topped Dock Ellis and relievers, 6-2. The Reds had a 3-0 lead and looked unbeatable. The only bright spot for the Yanks were three hits by Thurman Munson, who was proving to be just about the only Yank the Redlegs couldn't handle. But the only thing Thurman and the rest of the Yanks were concerned with was winning game four, avoiding an embarrassing sweep, and getting back into the Series. They sent 19-game winner Ed Figueroa to the mound against the Reds' Gary Nolan.

The Yanks got a run in the first, but it didn't do much good. Cincy broke through for three in the third and it was all but over. They held a 3-2 lead going into their half of the ninth, then got four more to break the Yanks' backs. It ended at 7-2 and the Yankees were finished, swept, humiliated. People began calling the Redlegs one of the best teams ever. The Yankee players sulked and owner Steinbrenner fumed.

Overlooked in the romp was the accomplishment of Thurman Munson. Perhaps more than anyone, Thurman dug in to try to avoid a sweep. And in doing so he managed nine hits in 17 at bats for a .529 average and a pair of RBI's. It was the highest average ever compiled by a player on a losing team, and he also tied a record by getting six consecutive hits, four of them coming in the final game. Thurman had played his heart out and gained even more respect.

"But we didn't win. . . ." he murmured, among other things. As always, Thurman played to win. The rest didn't matter.

It was after the Series ended that the honors really rolled in. First, Thurman was named Most Valuable Player in the American League, an honor the Munson of old probably never would have expected. He'd have figured one of those flashy guys would have won it. That wasn't all. The *Sporting News* named him American League Player of the Year and the Associated Press named him catcher on the 1977 Major League All-Star team. He also made several American League all-star teams. It was Thurman's year, all right.

Of course, one little problem remained. The Yanks fell four games short of winning it all. That was four games they all wanted. Owner Steinbrenner decided to once again loosen his wallet and dip into the free agent market. This time he really went all out, pulling in the two most glamorous and talented players on the market.

The first was Don Gullett, the very pitcher who had beaten the Yanks in game one of the Series. Gullett played out his option with the Reds and signed with the Yanks for six years and nearly two million dollars.

And if that wasn't enough, Steinbrenner then went after the top hitter among the free agents, controversial Reggie Jackson.

It was common knowledge that wherever the highly emotional, but extremely talented Jackson played, there was trouble. Reggie liked to be top gun, needed respect and love from his teammates and fans to be happy. The story was that Steinbrenner called his captain, Thurman Munson, and asked his opinion on signing Jackson.

"Go get him," Thurman reportedly said.

That's what Steinbrenner did, signing Reggie to a five-year contract worth some $2,900,000. And in an attempt to insure harmony for the upcoming year, the Yankee owner invited Thurman to the press conference that introduced Reggie as a New York Yankee. Soon after, the Yankee owner picked up Paul Blair from the Orioles as outfield insurance, and also acquired shortstop Bucky Dent from the Chicago White Sox. Shortly into the season he got pitcher Mike Torrez from Oakland. By that time people were calling the Yanks "the best team money could buy."

But teams bought by large sums of money don't always win. It had failed before. When you're paying some players huge amounts, others are bound to become jealous. Yet Steinbrenner practically demanded the team to win, so the pressure was on, especially on Manager Billy Martin, who would have to keep all his big stars happy.

It didn't take long for the trouble to start, and from an unlikely source. Word began getting out that Thurman Munson was unhappy, that he felt Steinbrenner had not kept certain financial promises to him—namely that he'd be the highest paid Yankee. Third baseman Graig Nettles also felt he was underpaid, as did relief ace Sparky Lyle. Perhaps Nettles said it best.

"We're the guys who worked our butts off to bring the Yankees back to the top, now these other guys come in and reap the rewards."

To make matters worse, the team started badly. Catfish Hunter hurt a foot on opening day and was out. After he returned, he had arm trouble off and on all year. Gullett was also having arm problems, which would recur from time to time. As for the hitters, they just couldn't put it together.

One thing augered well, though. Munson and Jackson seemed to be getting along; becoming friends, in fact. But then the inevitable happened. A magazine article, which was prepared during spring training, finally hit the stands. In it, Jackson said some rather uncomplimentary things about Thurman to the effect that he, Jackson, was the man who would have to do it for the Yanks, not Munson. The way it came out in the magazine made it sound even worse than that.

It was the last straw. Thurman had been the acknowledged leader of the team for several years, and the article not only incensed him, but many of his teammates as well. The club quickly divided into Munson and Jackson factions as they continued to battle Boston and Baltimore for the A.L. East lead.

Thurman, in fact, was one of the few Yankees doing a consistent job at the plate, and as usual he was leading the team in runs batted in. Jackson, for all the hoopla, wasn't hitting, though he asserted himself from time to time with a clutch game-winner. But he wasn't doing it on an everyday basis.

Reggie began to feel he wasn't appreciated. Many of the fans, loyal to Munson, were booing him. He began to sulk, and clash with Manager Martin. The Yanks were beginning to be known as the most dissension-filled team since the Oakland A's of the early 1970s. But that team managed to win three straight world titles despite the in-fighting. And that club was also led by Reggie Jackson.

There was one thing after another. More than once the papers and media had Steinbrenner firing Martin, but Billy the Kid hung on. Jackson felt he should be batting fourth and Steinbrenner agreed, but Martin stubbornly insisted he'd make out the lineup card and kept Chris Chambliss in the cleanup spot. This seemed to make Jackson pout even more. Some players began to make sounds about playing elsewhere next season. And for the first time one of them was Thurman Munson.

"I wouldn't mind playing in Cleveland, near my home," said the Ohio-born Thurman. "Especially with all the stuff that's going on around here."

No one had ever thought of Thurman as anything but a Yankee, the man who followed Dickey, Berra, and Howard. But the battling Yanks of '77 could make anyone want to go elsewhere at one time or another.

Yet despite all the controversy and his obvious dislike of Jackson, Thurman kept pretty much quiet. He said he felt the magazine article was wrong, that Jackson should have kept his mouth shut, but as for bad-mouthing of his own, Thurman just didn't do it for the press. He just kept playing every day and tried to hold the Yanks together with his bat.

On June 18, the Yanks had a 36-28 mark and were 1½ games behind the Red Sox. They were playing the Sox in Boston, a game shown on national television. Late in the game a Boston player lofted a pop to right. Jackson came in lackadaisically, and the ball fell in front of him for a hit. Martin thought he wasn't hustling, and in mid-inning sent Paul Blair to right and pulled Jackson from the game.

Reggie was humiliated before millions of fans and let Martin know it. With the cameras tuned in, the two began shoving in the dugout. Suddenly Martin snapped and it took three players to keep Billy from tearing into Jackson. Now it looked as if the Yank split could never be repaired.

But somehow the team hung in there, with the usual apologies and rumors about Martin's firing. The Yanks, Sox, and Orioles continued taking turns at winning streaks. By August 10, the Yanks had a 61-49 mark, but they had fallen to third place, five games behind the leading Bosox. Something had to be done.

Finally it was Thurman Munson and another veteran, Lou Pinella, who went to see Martin. The nonsense had to stop if the team was going to win. The players talked for several hours with their manager about the club and its problems. And they indirectly suggested something to Billy. Give Jackson a shot at the cleanup spot.

Martin must have figured he had nothing to lose, and the next day Jackson was installed in the number four slot where he stayed the rest of the year. And suddenly, the team began to win.

They began to win for several reasons. One was that Jackson responded to getting his way. Reggie does have an enormous talent, and he went on one of his patented tears that lasted right until the end of the season. In addition, Thurman, Chambliss, Nettles, Rivers, and Pinella were all having fine seasons at the plate. Plus the addition of Mike Torrez and the emergence of young lefthander Ron Guidry gave the staff two starters who won consistently the last two months while the big names, Hunter and Gullett, suffered with arm problems. In addition, Sparky Lyle was having his greatest year out of the bullpen and Dick Tidrow was doubling successfully as an effective reliever and reliable spot starter. The Yanks had finally put it together. "The best team money could buy" was winning.

From the switch of Jackson to cleanup on August 10, the Yanks won 39 of their next 52 to finish at 100-62 and nail down the flag, though the tough Red Sox hung in there until the second to last day of the year. But the club had won again, despite the dissension and the in-fighting, the threats and requests for trades. They won. But they still had two more hurdles to get over. The first was to meet the Kansas City Royals once more in the playoffs. The Royals remembered the past season's loss and were vowing revenge.

As for the individual Yank performances, well, they were very, very good. Jackson's tear resulted in one of his best seasons. He hit .286, slammed 32 homers, and led the club with 110 runs batted in. He also swiped 17 bases. Third baseman Nettles had another fine year, with career highs of 37 homers and 107 RBI's. Chambliss had 17 four baggers, 90 ribbys, and a .287 mark. Rivers hit .326 with 12 homers and 69 RBI's as the leadoff man, while Lou Pinella batted .330 playing regularly the second half of the year. The team also got good mileage out of mid-season pickup Cliff Johnson. The big guy had 12 homers and 31 RBI's in just 56 games.

Thurman had slumped a bit in late August and early September, his average falling below .300. It also looked as if he wouldn't get his 100 RBI's. But he dug in the last couple of weeks to finish with a .308 mark, 18 homers, and an even 100 RBI's. It was his third straight .300, 100 RBI season. And only Chambliss had come to bat more often for the team.

Guidry and Figueroa led the pitchers with 16 wins

each, Torrez had 14 as a Yankee (three more with Oakland), Gullett managed 14 despite the arm problems, while Lyle had 13 wins and 26 saves (he would later win the Cy Young Award as the best pitcher in the American League), and Tidrow notched 11 victories.

But the Royals wouldn't be pushovers, and they proved it in game one as lefty Paul Splittorff bested Don Gullett and relievers, 7-2. Gullett also reinjured his shoulder and was thought to be lost for the season.

In game two the Yanks got even, 6-2, with Ron Guidry doing his thing. But the real fun started in the sixth inning when the Royals Hal McRae took out Willie Randolph with a rugged block at second base, breaking up a double play.

The Yanks fumed, and in their half of the inning Thurman flashed his spikes sliding into third base, and he and the Royals George Brett looked at each other menacingly.

"I slid late just to let him know I was there," Thurm admitted, afterwards. "If I'd have wanted to hit him, I'd have hit him. My argument isn't with George Brett. The guy I want to get is McRae. He better stay away from me. I told him so. He's been trying to hurt people for eight years."

McRae, of course, insisted the block was clean and that he'd do it again. Munson, as Yankee captain and a gritty competitor, felt compelled to take a stand. So the flames had been kindled; the rivalry between the two clubs increased even more.

The scene shifted back to Kansas City, and the Royals took game three, 6-2, behind their 20-game-winner Dennis Leonard's four hitter. The Yanks were a game away from elimination. It didn't look good. What made it worse, not one of the big Yankee hitters was doing beans.

Ed Figueroa started game four against ex-Yank Larry Gura. Neither starting pitcher had good stuff. In the fourth inning the Yanks had a 5-4 lead, but the Royals had runners at first and third with two out. That's when Sparky Lyle came in. He retired George Brett to end the inning, then buzzed through the Royals the rest of the way, allowing just two hits. Late in the game Thurman hit a sacrifice fly for an insurance run, making it 6-4, and that's the way it ended.

"I was kind of afraid," Thurm said, "after I drove in the sixth run, because Sparky doesn't know what to do with a two-run lead. He gets flustered out there."

He was kidding, of course, but there was still a fifth game to play, and it would be the tough Paul Splittorff again. The Yanks countered with Ron Guidry, starting with just two days rest. There was added turmoil when Manager Martin benched Jackson for the final game. Reggie hadn't been hitting and never hit Splittorff very well. Once again the star outfielder's pride was hurt and the players divided, pro and con Martin. With the pennant at stake, the Yankee clubhouse was again filled with dissension.

Guidry just couldn't do it on two days rest. He gave up two runs in the first, an inning also marked by a fight between George Brett and Nettles on a slide at third. Then in the Yankee third, Rivers singled, stole second, and scored on Thurman's single. But the Royals got another in their half of the third to lead, 3-1, and sent Guidry to the showers. In came Mike Torrez, who had gone five and two-thirds in the third game loss. He came in on one day's rest. If he didn't have it, the Yanks were really in trouble.

Fortunately, he did, and the score stayed the same into the eighth. Then Willie Randolph singled, Thurman struck out, but Pinella singled. Up came Reggie Jackson, pinch hitting for Cliff Johnson. With the

pressure on, Reggie singled to center to make it 3-2.
But a great play by second baseman Frank White on a
smash by Chambliss prevented further scoring. The
Yanks had one more chance or their season would be
over.

Paul Blair led off the ninth against K.C. ace Dennis
Leonard, who was brought in to save it. But Blair
poked a single to center and Roy White walked. Lefty
Larry Gura came in to pitch, and Mickey Rivers
singled to right, scoring Blair and tying the game.
Randolph then hit a sacrifice fly off Mark Littell, the
third pitcher in the inning, and the Yankees had a 4-3
lead! When Pinella hit a grounder to third and Brett
threw it away, another run scored and the Yanks led,
5-3, in what looked like a miracle finish.

It was, as Sparky Lyle calmly retired the Royals
in the ninth. The Yankees were American League
champions once again. Two years in a row they had
beaten the Royals in the final inning of the final game,
and you can't cut it much closer than that. For the
moment, peace and joy prevailed in the Yankee
clubhouse. But the Los Angeles Dodgers awaited
them in the World Series, so the final battle had yet to
begin.

There had been many classic Yankee-Dodger
battles in the past, going back to Brooklyn days, and
this could yet be another. Martin pulled a surprise by
naming Don Gullett his starter in game one, the sore
arm supposedly better.

Both Gullett and Dodger starter Don Sutton
pitched well. The Dodgers got a pair of runs in the
first before Gullett settled down. In the bottom of the
inning singles by Munson, Jackson, and Chambliss
made it 2-1. Thurman's hit was his seventh straight in
World Series play, six coming the year before against
Cincinnati—a new major league record. He fanned in

the third to break the string, but in the eighth he slammed a hit-and-run double to left to score Randolph with the run that made it 3-2. The Dodgers tied it in the eighth, but Sparky Lyle was now on the mound, and he held them into the 12th when the Yankees won it on a double by Randolph and single by Paul Balir. The New Yorkers had a one game lead.

Hoping to rest his tired pitching staff, Manager Martin decided to gamble on sore-armed Catfish Hunter in game two. That started the turmoil again. Jackson publicly second-guessed Martin in the newspapers and Billy burned. So did Thurman Munson who, for one of the few times all years, voluntarily jumped into the fray.

"I've had it with this stuff," Thurm said. "I've got five more games to worry about this, then I'm gone. I've been made a heavy all year. But you never saw any article about me criticizing any teammate or manager."

Thurm was reiterating his desire to be traded, to get out of the tension-filled Yankee situation. Then when the Dodgers, behind Burt Hooten, bombed Catfish and the Yanks, 6-1, to tie the Series, it seemed that Jackson's criticism was justified. But Thurm said Hunter actually had good velocity, he just hung some sliders that the Dodgers hit out. And it did give the staff some extra rest, so perhaps sacrificing that game was worth it.

It seemed so in game three, when Mike Torrez recovered from a shaky start and went the route, beating the Dodgers, 5-3, out in L.A., to give the Yanks a 2-1 lead. Thurm had a hit and RBI in that one, as did Jackson.

Now the Yanks were happy again, apologies made. Thurman was singing in the clubhouse and asking, "Did I ever say I wanted to be traded to Cleveland?"

Another Yankee concluded, "Reggie is disruptive!" And a third said, "Who can tell around here. Things change every 30 seconds."

Then came game four and young Ron Guidry took over. The slim, but hard-throwing lefty handcuffed the Dodgers on four hits and the Yanks won, 4-2, with Jackson warming up with a double and home run. The Yanks led, 3-1, and finally seemed to be in a commanding position.

It was Gullett and Sutton again in game five, and this time Gullett didn't have it. The Dodgers bombed the Yanks, 10-4, but in the eighth inning Munson and Jackson hit back-to-back homers. It seems as if the two stars were linked to each other, even in defeat. Though the Yanks still led, three games to two, the rumors flew again.

This time there was a report that Jackson would refuse to play for the Yanks in '78 if Martin was still manager. Jackson called the story an "out and out lie!" The story also claimed Munson and Pinella asked Steinbrenner to fire Martin back in July. Now Thurm was angry because he had been one of Martin's strongest supporters all year. Would the strife never end?

Nope. Martin then named Mike Torrez to start again in game six. This made Ed Figueroa demand a trade since he felt he should start, despite some hand problems. Roy White, the veteran Yankee, also was burning at the fact that Lou Pinella had taken his place in left. Mickey Rivers was always chirping about being traded, his latest theme being he wanted to play in sunny California again. It just kept on and on. Plus Torrez was unsigned and threatened to become a free agent after the season ended, win or lose.

Then, before the sixth game, Martin got a vote a confidence, a $50,000 bonus and the assurance that he'd be back next year no matter what the outcome of the Series. Apparently Steinbrenner and President Gabe Paul wanted to stop all those Martin-being-fired stories. So the Yanks went into the sixth game with all these things on their minds, Torrez facing the winner of game two, Burt Hooten.

The Dodgers got a pair in the first, but in the Yank second Reggie walked and Chambliss belted a long, two-run homer. Tie game. In the third the Dodgers got another to break the tie.

Then in the Yankee fourth Thurman singled and Jackson promptly lined the first pitch into the right field stands, giving the Yanks a 4-3 lead.

Hooten got the boot, and Elias Sosa came in. The Yanks made it 5-3 on a sacrifice fly by Pinella. In the fifth, Rivers singled, and two outs later Jackson pickled Sosa's first pitch into the stands for his second homer and a 7-3 lead. The fans at Yankee Stadium went wild.

Then in the eighth inning Reggie came up again, this time facing knuckleballer Charlie Hough. Again he went for the first pitch, hitting a towering drive into the centerfield bleachers, his third homer of the game, a mammoth shot that tied a record set by the one and only Babe Ruth. It was also his fifth homer of the Series, setting a brand new record for himself.

The Dodgers managed another run in the ninth, but Torrez closed the door and it was over. The Yanks were World Champs, for the first time in 15 years. And the hero, after everything that had happened all season long, was Reggie Jackson, who gave a slugging display the likes of which had never been seen before in the Series. Reggie had nine hits in 20 trips for a .450 average, five homers, and eight RBI's.

The only other Yankee to hit over .300 was, you guessed it, Thurman Munson. Though overshadowed by Jackson, Thurman again played clutch ball, with eight hits in 25 AB's for a .320 mark. He had a homer and three RBI's.

In the clubhouse everyone was celebrating, over-joyed. All the former enemies hugged each other, but under the surface the caldron was still boiling. A smiling Munson yelled at Series MVP Jackson:

"See you next year, wherever I might be!"

"You'll be back," Jackson answered.

"Not me," Munson said, still smiling.

"You'll be here next year," Reggie answered. "We'll all be here!"

But as the long, tension-filled year finally ended, Thurman said, "I can't go through another year like this, no way. The Series is going to hit me in a couple of days. But I was happier when we won the playoffs, just because of all the stuff we've been through and being under the gun all the time. I'm tired now. I'm happy it's over."

The Yankees, of course, announced they would only make trades that would help the club. And when someone asked President Gabe Paul about Thurman's desire to go to Cleveland, Paul answered:

"I understand his desire to be near his home. But we would not entertain any thought of trading Thurman Munson unless the Yankees could benefit from such a transaction. It would be pretty hard to do that."

Ironically, that December, Paul himself wound up in Cleveland. He resigned from the Yankees and joined the Indians as part of a new ownership, and would be responsible for rebuilding the team. And oh how he'd love to have Thurman Munson!

So as the 1978 season neared, Thurman's fate was still uncertain. It would, however, be difficult to imagine him wearing another uniform. The Yanks did lose

Series hero Mike Torrez. He spurned a Yankee bid and signed as a free agent with rival Boston, a strange circumstance. But the Bombers signed a free agent of their own, ace righthanded reliever Rich Gossage, who had been with Pittsburgh. They figured their bullpen would now be untouchable.

At any rate, it is safe to assume the team will be changing again, to some degree. The talent is certainly there to keep the club on top for a long time to come, and that's another reason it's hard to see Munson leaving. The Cleveland situation has been unstable for some time.

In addition, Thurman now has the recognition and respect he always craved. He's always been a winner, and now he's on a winning team. And don't forget, he's part of a long tradition, and despite the cold, dispassionate, businesslike stance the game and many of its stars have taken today, tradition still means something. It's not every catcher who can be part of a great line and who fully deserves his place among them.

Let's face it. They'll all be remembered: Dickey, Berra, Howard, and Thurman Munson. Winners all!

★ LOU BROCK ★

★ It was still early in the 1973 baseball season, but Lou Brock was worried. The fleet leftfielder of the St. Louis Cardinals didn't feel he was running well. He was rapidly approaching his thirty-fourth birthday, and suddenly the stolen bases weren't coming.

Stolen bases had been a major part of Lou Brock's game for some time. In fact, he had set a major league record by stealing fifty or more bases for eight consecutive seasons, beginning in 1965. So he was already regarded as one of the master base thiefs of all time, as well as an outstanding all-around player—a "money player," a clutch performer who knew how to win. Yet despite all this, Brock was worried.

"I had been thrown out thirteen of the first twenty-three times I ran," he recalls, "and I was getting all kinds of negative vibes running through my head. I was almost thirty-four years old, and I figured I had slowed up. I thought I couldn't run anymore. I remember one day I was stealing and I just stopped. Stopped cold in the middle of the baseline. I thought I heard the batter hit a foul ball, but he hadn't even swung, and I was a sitting duck."

The incident put another dent in Brock's rapidly ebbing confidence. After eight seasons as a superthief, the best base runner in the majors, Lou felt it all slipping away. And he had always maintained that once the skills began to go, he'd quit rather than hang on like so many other players. For the first time since he broke in with the Cubs back in 1962, Lou Brock thought the end was in sight.

Cardinal Executive Vice President and General Manager Bing Devine remembers that time well.

"Lou developed a state of mind that year," recalls Devine, "because everybody—and most of them in a respectful way—was telling him, 'Look, at 34, don't expect to be what you were from 28-34. You're really past your prime and past your peak and you're gonna have to recognize and accept it. You're still gonna be a good ballplayer, but you're not going be as outstanding as you've been.'

"With all these people saying it, Lou just kind of made up his own mind and accepted it. Then one day he just sat down and decided he had to turn around his state of mind, stop listening to other people and be positive instead of negative."

A chance meeting with former base-stealing king Maury Wills didn't hurt either. Maury was a sportscaster in 1973, still an astute observer of the game, and as soon as he saw Lou he knew what was troubling him.

"Maury didn't mince words," said Lou. "He told me right away to just keep running and not to count the times I was caught. I took his advice and with my own new attitude, pretty soon it all started coming together again."

It came together, all right. Brock finished the 1973 season with 70 steals, good enough to lead the league once again, and the second best total of his career. He obviously hadn't slowed up. In fact, by season's end, people were saying he was better than ever.

Yet no one suspected what was to come in 1974. If anything, most baseball people felt Brock would slow down somewhat. After all, he'd be nearly thirty-five years old, and at that age it isn't easy stealing 60 or 70 bases. Most reasoned that the wear and tear would be too great. Brock's skills might enable him to get another 50 or so, but he was too smart a player to push it too hard. He wouldn't put his body on the line for another 10 or 15 steals. He'd pace himself more then ever before. Veteran ballplayers usually do that at age thirty-five. They just can't go every day like they used to ten years earlier.

But like other very great players who have performed well beyond their years, Lou Brock has an enormous amount of pride; he is driven by some inner fire burning deep within his soul. In fact, Bing Devine compared him with another Cardinal great who was, in this respect, much the same.

"I've said all along," explained Devine, "that Lou followed in the footsteps of Stan Musial as our superstar among everyday players. I say 'everyday' so as not to exclude Bob Gibson, who was a pitcher. But neither Musial nor Brock had dominating personalities. They're not really extremely outgoing, particularly as ballplayers. But they both showed leadership qualities through their ability, and their play, and their condition. Neither was a gung-ho team man, like Pete Rose, for example. Their intensity came completely from within."

So in 1974, Lou Brock fooled them all. Taking up where he left off in 1973, he ran, and ran, and ran. By midseason he already had his 50 steals, and people were now beginning to talk about a new record. They were also wondering if Brock's body could take the beating.

He showed them, not by slowing down or pacing himself, but by running even more. In a weekend series against the Phillies in early August, the 5'-11",

170-pounder not only banged out 10 hits in 17 at bats but also swiped 8 bases in 9 attempts. Talk of a new record increased, and so did Brock's pace. By the time he got his hundredth and hundred-and-first steals (against the Mets on September 6), it was obvious that only an injury could prevent Brock from breaking the mark.

Steal number 104, against the Phils, not only tied the record but also gave Brock a National League career mark of 739 steals. By the time the season ended, the baseball world stood in awe of the thirty-five-year-old superstar. At an age when most players were looking toward retirement, Lou Brock had set an amazing record. In 153 games, he had stolen 118 bases!

It was a truly momentous feat, made even greater by considering Brock's age and the cases of baseball's other premier base stealers, Wills and the immortal Ty Cobb.

Wills was approaching thirty when he swiped his 104 in 1962, while Cobb was not yet twenty-nine the year he pilfered 96, way back in 1915. And both men testified to the bumps and bruises, the toll that stealing so many bases took on their bodies. They were constantly nursing scrapes and sores; running on fragile, tired legs; finishing the season nearly exhausted.

Yet Brock, some six years or so older than the other two, finished as fast or faster than he started, missing just nine games, and six of those were the result of a shoulder injury suffered in the outfield. The steals seemed to come easy.

The answer lies in his approach to base running. Brock's approach is distinctly different from both Cobb's and Wills'. Ty Cobb was the best ballplayer of his generation, and in the minds of many, the best of all time. He was a fiery soul, an intense competitor who would do anything to win a ball game. He made himself a base stealer and studied every possible way of getting an advantage once he reached base. And he reached base more than anyone else, getting more than 4,000 hits during his long career.

As a base runner he was a terror. He had better than average speed, which he used to the maximum, but he also let it be known that his spikes would come in high if the situation called for it. Not that Cobb was a dirty player. He once said he only spiked two players intentionally during his playing days. But he also said that baseball was "an unrelenting war of nerves," and he used that psychology to instill a kind of fear in opposing players. Fear of Cobb's spikes did as much damage as the spikes themselves.

But base running was still a bruising business for Cobb. There were plenty of head-on collisions, and to avoid them, Cobb used a variety of slides and maneuvers.

"The whole secret of sliding is to make your move at the last possible second," Cobb once said. "When I went in there I wanted to see the whites of the fielder's eyes. I liked to come straight at him, then collapse right or left after perhaps faking the other way.

"Sometimes I'd deliberately slide wide, go past the bag, then reach back and hook the outside corner with my trailing toe. And there were times when I'd go even further past and reach back with my hand to get the bag."

Combining all this with the rough, unkempt infields of the day, many of which were loaded with pebbles and small stones, and Cobb was one beat-up ballplayer by the time August and September rolled around. Guts and courage kept him going, but his body took a terrific beating.

There were many other top base runners in Cobb's

day. That's the way the game was played. But when Maury Wills came up in 1959, the home run had already taken over the running game. The base stealing title in the 1950s was often won with under 30 steals. Yet that didn't deter Wills. He went about the business of learning to run the bases against National League pitchers. In his second season, 1960, he took his first base-stealing crown, with 50 thefts. Two years later he would set a new standard with 104. So with Wills leading the way, base running began to reappear, and once again many young players began running.

Wills was no one-shot wonder. He reached the majors later than most, but he had a second big year in 1965, with 94 steals, when he was already thirty-three. Wills was a lot like Ty Cobb in that he played the game at a high intensity and pulled out all stops to steal a base or help in a victory. At 5'-10", 165-pounds, his body took a pounding from his slides and competitive tactics. In fact, after his record-breaking 1962 season, he fell off in 40 steals in 1963; and after his 94 steals in 1965, he dropped to 38. It might have been the pounding.

Lou Brock has avoided that kind of thing. He is perhaps the most consistent base stealer of all time, as his record of 12 consecutive 50-steal seasons attests. He has perhaps the most clinical approach to stealing of all the great ones. He does it the same way every time. He uses the same slide, which happens to be the safest and least damaging, and in that way avoids some of the bruising pitfalls that made stealing a painful proposition to the others.

"I saw Maury Wills run quite often," Brock says. "He used the hook slide almost exclusively. That means he's always going for the corner of the base. It's a beautiful but damaging slide, because a larger portion of your body—legs, rump, arms, elbows, and even back—can make contact with the ground. I always use the straight-in, or 'pop-up', slide. That way, just my calves absorb any real contact or punishment."

It all sounds pretty simple: Brock gets to first, Brock takes off, Brock slides straight into second, Brock has another stolen base. Very neat and clean. But although Brock's technique is clinical, it's a technique that has been developed, step by step, for many years.

"It's been years of practice and torture for me," Brock said during his record-breaking season. "First of all, it's learning to read the pitchers. Every base runner must do this if he expects to steal successfully. By reading the pitcher he knows when to run and when he can get his best jump.

"This is directly related to leading. The amount of lead a runner takes is related to confidence and his ability to read the pitcher. He's got to know he can get back and must know just how far he can go before he's in no-man's land, the point of no return. So it's essential to establish an association with first base. You can't watch the pitcher and keep looking back to the base. You never beat a pitcher by guessing where you are. This is a precise business, with no place for error.

"The initial thrust is another absolute must. A runner can practice and improve upon this. He's got to be able to move out and be at maximum speed within ten steps or so. It's a matter of power and thrust and can be achieved through hard work."

These are still all basics, basics that not every fast runner can achieve, but basics nevertheless. After that, it's a matter of further refinement. That is where the real science comes in, where the men are separated from the boys. And this is where Lou Brock is a total artist.

"I have a decided advantage over the pitcher," Lou says, "because I can change my stealing technique, but a pitcher's motion is mechanical. He cannot alter it without risking injury to his arm. By using varying lengths and styles of lead and takeoffs, I minimize detection of my plans.

"All pitchers fall into four broad catagories. The anatomy of their bodies dictates what moves they have to make. I rate moves as fast, quick, moderate, and slow. Believe it or not, a pitcher can be slow and quick. So you've got to learn it all.

"Another factor is the stuff the pitcher has. If you have a sinker ball pitcher, the catcher will have to come up more before he gets the ball off. But when there's a fastballer, say like Tom Seaver, on the mound, the ball just zings in there, and the catcher is ready to get the peg off a split-second sooner. And that can be the difference."

Both Brock and Maury Wills acknowledge that it was more difficult stealing more than 100 bases in 1974 than it was in 1962. Says Wills:

"In some ways the record was more difficult for Lou than it was for me. At the time I broke Cobb's mark everyone was home run conscious, and the pitchers weren't used to keeping runners close to first. I could get some pretty good leads.

"But after I stole 104 the game kind of changed. Pitchers started working on keeping the good base runners close to first and not letting them get a huge jump."

Brock looks at it in terms of the catchers. "When I first came up there wasn't that much stealing and the catchers weren't ready. Not that many of them could get the ball down to second quickly, and not many throws came in low and on the bag. But with more players running in the last years, the young catchers are ready. They can all throw and welcome the challenge of cutting down the top base runners."

"Challenge." That's a word with which Lou Brock is very familiar. He's known about it ever since his childhood, when the primary challenge was simply to survive.

Lou Brock was born on June 18, 1939, in El Dorado, Arkansas. But when he was still very young, his parents separated, and his mother packed up the family's belongings and took her children to Mer Rouge, Louisiana, a small town some ninety miles southeast of El Dorado. Mrs. Brock had relatives in Mer Rouge and figured she could get work there more easily.

Since there were nine children, in the Brock family, it wasn't easy for Mrs. Brock or for Lou and his brothers and sisters. Lou's childhood filled him with thoughts and images that were not only difficult to overcome, but also left him with scars that may never totally heal.

"You grow up insecure about everything," he once admitted. "You grow up ashamed of your mouth, ashamed of your nose, ashamed of your skin. It takes a long time to overcome that."

Being black and poor—and living in a small Southern town—helped formulate these images on Lou's mind, as it did with many other black youngsters. They had no idea of what the world was really like.

"When I was a kid that's the way I thought everybody lived," Lou says. "I didn't know there was such a thing as a steady job. I thought everybody had a job for a day or two and got another one."

It was largely that way for Mrs. Brock and many of

her friends and relatives. They did whatever work they could to support their families. As Lou remembers:

"My mother did what all black women did to support their children. She scrubbed floors and cleaned up garbage."

Unpleasant memories, surely. But no more unpleasant than life itself was in Mer Rouge. It was a hot, dusty town with not much to do during the long summer months, as well as the rest of the year. The boys played some ball, but went about it half-heartedly. There was nothing and no one to motivate them. They just kind of drifted aimlessly from one thing to another, trying to find a small measure of fun and something that would hold their interest.

School didn't do much in that area. Lou remembers how it was when he started.

"They make a big fuss about busing now," he says. "Well, when I was a kid they bused us for miles, way out of town, past a dozen white schools, to the black school. Nobody talked about that kind of busing."

But Lou remembers. He remembers watching out the window of the bus and wondering what life was all about. Despite his meager, almost mechanical day-to-day existence, he sometimes had visions of a better life.

"As a kid I wondered what life meant for me, what life had in store for me," he recalls. "When I looked at everything around me it wasn't a pretty picture. I saw people unemployed, depressed. At night sometimes I'd lay in bed and look up at the stars, saying to myself: 'There has to be *something* better for me. All right, how do I go about getting it?'"

That was the problem. Getting it, whatever it was, seemed like a mere pipe dream. Wherever Lou thought of turning, the road seemed blocked by the poverty, depression, and general aimlessness of his small world.

Then one day, when Lou was in junior high school and the boredom seemed worse than ever, he decided to have some fun. He rolled up a spitball and fired it at one of his friends. Only he missed. Instead, it hit his teacher smack in the forehead!

Lou's teacher was furious, but she knew that a tongue lashing—or even a physical beating—probably wouldn't have a lasting effect on the youngster. So she devised another kind of punishment. She sent Lou to the school library to do some research work on the careers of Jackie Robinson, Don Newcombe, Stan Musial, and Joe DiMaggio. Lou remembers what happened next.

"I didn't know a thing about baseball then, but I started reading anyway. I quickly found that these guys not only ran after a little white ball, but they got paid big money for it. So much money, in fact, that I couldn't even read the figures. So I took the book back to my class and asked the teacher what one of the numbers was. She told me it was one hundred thousand dollars!

"I couldn't believe it. One hundred thousand dollars—just for chasing the little white ball. From that day on I wanted to be a pro ballplayer. From that day on I knew how to get that something better. Through sport, the one time in a ghetto kid's life where everybody played by the same rules."

Lou hadn't played any serious ball before, and he had a lot of catching up to do. But as soon as he reached Union High School in Mer Rouge, he went out for baseball. He ended up playing four years of baseball and three of basketball at Union, and he really worked at it for the first time.

It didn't take long for Lou to learn he could excel. He was a guard and forward on the basketball team, pitched and played the outfield in baseball. He was fast even then, but since almost all of the players had real good speed, he didn't think about using it in any special kind of way. Besides, power was the name of the big-league game then, and Lou worked to be a stronger hitter.

The work seemed to be paying off. Lou never batted under .350 in high school, and as a switch-hitter his senior year he compiled a .536 batting average. Things were looking up. Maybe his dream wasn't so unreal after all.

Now came the time for a big decision. It wasn't a real difficult one to make. If Lou wanted to be a ballplayer and prepare himself for life at the same time, he'd have to go to college.

The tough part was finding a college that would offer him a scholarship. There was no way he could pay his own way. And in this area he found sports weren't equal. There were many more scholarships available for white athletes. The integrated schools always had more openings for whites, and the black schools didn't have that much money to pass around. Besides, there weren't as many black colleges to pick from.

Lou wrote letters and made applications to almost every school in the South. The responses were all negative. Only one held out any hope. That was Southern University, an all-black school located in Baton Rouge, Louisiana. Southern didn't make any promises to Lou but asked him to come down and visit the campus.

It was a 160-mile trip, and since Lou had no money, he was forced to hitchhike. But he got there and liked what he saw. More importantly, school officials liked him. They couldn't offer him a scholarship right then, but they did promise him work to help pay tuition.

Lou entered Southern in 1958. In the fall he started

studies and a job as a part-time janitor and grasscutter. It was a rough grind, but Lou made it through to the spring and baseball time. Once again there was a test, and this time Lou almost didn't make it.

"I gave myself two weeks to make the team," he recalls. "I worked for two weeks hard as I could but the coach never took one look at me. I guess he was looking at the guys he knew and the ones who were on scholarship. But I stayed on anyway, kept practicing every minute I could. Then I lost my janitorial job. The little money I had was gone and to eat, I started visiting friends' houses right around mealtimes.

"On the field I tried to do everything to impress the coach. If I was playing left field and a ball was hit to right, I'd try to run it down. This kept up for another month. Then one day I just collapsed from exhaustion, right on the field."

His collapse forced the coach to notice Lou. The next time he got in the batting cage he knew the coach was watching. Weak as he was, he hit four straight balls over the fence. He was on the team.

There was a lot of learning for Lou that freshman year at Southern. He was still mastering fundamentals, since he had taken up the game later in life than most of the other boys. As a result he was a part-time player and hit under .200. But just being on the team was enough. It helped Lou straighten out his head and look to the future with optimism once more.

When he came back the next year, everything seemed to fall into place. Lou purposely took the hardest courses, concentrating on math (a subject area he felt could help him later in life). At various times during his stay at Southern, he wanted to be an architect or a teacher, but baseball changed all that.

Lou had scholarship money that year, and during the season he earned all Southwestern Athletic Conference honors with a .542 batting average. The improvement was amazing as more and more of Lou's natural talents became visible. He was expected to be even better in the 1961 season, but something happened to change all that: the Chicago Cubs offered the young outfielder a bonus of $30,000 to sign with them.

To Lou, who had known nothing but poverty all his life, it was a staggering sum. It was also a chance to pursue his dream. He now had the confidence and felt he could make it. So he quickly decided to leave Southern and sign with the Cubs.

The Cubs figured Lou would need some seasoning. They wanted to see what he'd do against other pros and assigned him to St. Cloud, Minnesota, in the Northern League. They figured if he did well during the 1961 season, they'd move him up a notch or two to one of their top minor league clubs. The only thing they didn't figure on was just how well Brock would perform.

In fact, Brock surprised the entire Northern League by burning it up from start to finish. He slammed out 181 hits in 501 at bats to win the batting title with a .361 mark. He also led the league in runs scored with 117, in doubles with 33, in put-outs with 277, and in hits with 181. In addition, he slammed out six triples, showed good power with 14 homers, and drove in 82 runs. And on top of all that he swiped 38 bases, using his exceptional speed and a little finesse. He played his first four major league games at the end of the 1961 season, and in 1962 he came to the majors to stay.

The Cubs did not have a powerhouse team when Brock joined them in 1962. There was room for young players, and Lou knew he had a good chance to crack the starting lineup. But although Lou knew he had speed, he thought he could make more of a contribution to the club through power.

"Maybe it was because there was so much emphasis on the home run then," he recalls, "and that's where I thought the money was. Or maybe it was because everyone had speed on my Southern University teams. But when I came to the majors, I really didn't think of myself as a base stealer. I felt I had good power and had always batted clean-up, or in one of the other power spots, so stealing bases wasn't on my mind at all."

But making good was on Lou's mind. He was so determined to stick in his first shot at a major league job that he put a lot of extra pressure on himself. A former teammate, pitcher Larry Jackson, remembers young Lou well.

"Lou just wasn't at all relaxed when he first came to the Cubs," said Jackson. "He was so tense that it seemed as if he'd break out in a big sweat just putting on his uniform. He was making it even tougher for himself. And there were still things he had to learn. He knew the mechanics of sliding, for instance, but didn't always know when to start his slide. Sometimes he'd slide late and tear the bag right out of the ground. He was still finding out how to play the game."

Lou was also having trouble in the outfield. His great speed made up for some other deficiencies, but he had some trouble picking up base hits and making a quick decision on where to throw the ball.

Yet he had enough natural ability to see considerable action. Playing mostly right field, Lou was in 123 games as a rookie. The stats weren't bad. He batted .263 with 114 hits in 434 at bats. He had 24 doubles, 7 triples, 9 homers, and 35 RBIs. With his speed he swiped 16 bases, but it wasn't a real part of his game.

The next year was more of the same. Brock was a regular, appearing in 148 games, and helped his team. Only the team was never in contention for the league title, so there wasn't really any pressure on the players. So from that standpoint, Lou didn't really improve, because his statistics were nearly the same as his rookie year. He hit just .258 with 9 homers and 37 RBIs. He managed 24 steals, but he also struck out 122 times.

His problems in the field continued. One rival player said, "Every ball hit toward Brock is an adventure," and an opposing manager claimed, "Brock double-dribbles everything hit his way." Some of the writers and fans of the Cubs wondered if Brock would ever improve or whether he'd be just another ballplayer with good speed and an equal penchant for making mistakes.

Brock must have been wondering as well. After all, once he dedicated himself to baseball and became established in the game he had always been a star—in high school, college, and his one season in the minor leagues. It had been almost too easy. Then suddenly, when given his chance in the bigs, he was blowing it. And when the 1964 season started the same way, Lou's mind began to boggle.

"I was down," Lou confessed. "I was confused about everything, and the more I got confused, the more I tried to analyze the situation, the more I thought about it. And that just added to the confusion."

In mid-June of 1964, Lou was again hovering around .250. He wasn't really contributing much to the Cub cause. He had only 2 homers and 14 RBI's in 215 at-bats, and had stolen just 10 bases. His leading statistic was his 14 errors in the outfield, which seemed to indicate his ineptitude on the picket line was growing worse. No wonder Lou was down. Yet neither he nor anyone else could know then that in just a few short months he would be the central figure in one of the most fantastic turnarounds in baseball history.

Lou certainly could not be considered a hot piece of baseball property in June of 1964. Yet there was a veteran baseball man very much interested in him. That was Johnny Keane, manager of the St. Louis Cardinals, a team then embroiled in a race for the National League pennant.

The Cards had a sound team, but Keane felt they were a player away from being outstanding. The need was for an outfielder, someone who could bat near the top of the order and create some action on the bases. At first glance it would seem that Brock had the raw ingredients, but he hadn't proven himself under fire. Yet Keane recalled a Cubs-Cards game earlier in the season when Brock had hit a hard grounder to third and had beaten a perfect throw to first. It was the kind of speed the Cardinal skipper was looking for. And on June 15, 1964, a trade was made that had everyone in St. Louis and Chicago buzzing.

The Cards announced that they had acquired Lou Brock in return for former 20-game winner, Ernie Broglio. Fans in both cities were vocal about it. Cardinal fans were disappointed; their team had traded a proven pitcher for an error-prone outfielder who batted .263 as a rookie and had gone downhill since. At the same time Cub fans thought they had found a pitcher who would bring many victories to the Windy City.

But it didn't quite work out that way. Manager Keane told Brock he'd play every day and installed him in left field and in the second spot in the batting order. Suddenly, an amazing change came over Lou Brock.

Playing for a contending team and knowing what his role was expected to be, Lou warmed to the task. He knew the Cards wanted his speed to get things started, to ignite rallies, to get on base and upset the opposition, to add another dimension to the St. Louis attack. And as soon as he realized this, he did some thinking and went about making an adjustment.

"When I first came to the majors, I still felt that power hitting was where the money was," Lou admitted. "But after a while I realized that power wasn't enough. You have to have *consistent* power, and I knew I didn't have the physical makeup to be a consistent long-ball hitter. So I had to make a choice. Do I go and try to develop myself as a power hitter or do I become a pest on the basepaths?

"I didn't really make a final decision until I was traded to the Cards. Then I took inventory of myself all over again, and that's when I became a base runner."

Not that Lou didn't have power. While still with the Cubs he once hit a home run into the centerfield bleachers of the old Polo Grounds in New York. The blast had to travel more than 460 feet, making Lou one of a rare handful of players to hit a homer in that distant no-man's land. But it wasn't enough to produce thirty to forty homers a year, and by 1964, Lou knew it. So he soon concentrated on developing the other phases of his game, harnessing the long-dormant talents concealed within his lithe body.

Once he began concentrating on base hits and getting on, Lou started pounding the ball with more consistency, and the hits came in droves. He forced himself to concentrate even more on studying the pitchers and their motions, and soon, whenever he had the chance, he started running—and making it. The stolen bases were coming, too, and the whole Cardinal attack seemed to come alive. Lou was providing the added dimension that Manager Keane had been looking for.

"It just took a few games for us to realize we did the right thing," Keane said. "Lou was a sparkplug right from the start. And he learned so quickly. Within a month he was as much a base-stealing threat as any player in the league."

The hits continued to come. Lou was a .300 hitter from the day he joined the team, and the Cards quickly surged toward the top of the league. By August, Brock was surging toward a .300 batting average, and that included his .251 with the Cubs.

Still, it all came down to the final weeks of the season. The Cards were playing well, but they trailed the Philadelphia Phillies by 6½ games with only 12 games left. It didn't look good, but no one expected a complete Philly collapse (the club dropped 10 straight games). At the same time the Cards kept winning, closing the gap and clinching the pennant on the final day of the season.

The team had made a great comeback, yet in a sense, its comeback had to rank behind that of Lou Brock. After joining the Cards in June, Brock spent the rest of the season as a .348 hitter, bringing his overall average up to .315. In addition, he reached the 200-hit plateau for the first time. He stroked out 30 doubles, 11 triples, and 14 homers during the season. He drove in 58 runs, 44 of them from the Cards. He scored 111 runs (81 of them for the Cards) and stole 43 bases. Of those steals, 33 came after he donned the Redbird uniform.

It was obvious to everyone concerned that Lou had become an entirely different ballplayer after the trade.

He had given the Cards what they needed—a ball-player who could get things started, a man who would get on base and then drive the pitcher to distraction with his base-running heroics. More often than not, Lou was at the hub of Redbird rallies; he was the catalyst that provided the spark for the other fine Cardinal hitters (Curt Flood, Ken Boyer, Bill White, Mike Shannon, and Tim McCarver). He fit in beautifully, and now he was an integral part of a championship team.

Then came the World Series, and here the Cards had a tough nut to crack. They'd be facing the New York Yankees—the Yankees of Mantle, Maris, Tresh, Pepitone, Ford, Richardson, Kubek, Howard, Stottlemyre, etc. Injury and age would begin to take their toll on the Yanks the following year, but 1964 represented the Bombers' fifth consecutive American League pennant and they were heavy favorites to win the Series.

It was a hard-fought Series from start to finish. The Yanks knew it wouldn't be easy when the Cards bombed them, 9-5, in the opening game. During that game, the Yanks also lost the services of ace pitcher Whitey Ford, who developed a sore arm, for the remainder of the series. But the New Yorkers came back behind Mel Stottlemyre to take the second game, 8-3, beating Card ace Bob Gibson in the process.

The teams split the next two, the Yanks winning number three, 2-1, and St. Louis taking the fourth, 4-3. So far, it had been a frustrating series for Lou. He had a single, a double, and two RBI's in the first game; but then he went hitless in the next three. Being a young player, three hitless games could have finished him for the rest of the Series.

Fortunately, Lou wasn't that kind of player. He had two hits and an RBI in game five as the Cards won behind Gibson, 5-2. The Yanks bounced back to win the sixth, 8-3, but Lou was the Cardinal star with three hits. Now it all boiled down to a seventh and final game. Mel Stottlemyre would pitch against Bob Gibson.

The game was scoreless for three and one-half innings. Then, in the bottom of the fourth, the Cardinals broke the ice. Lou singled in the middle of a three-run rally. In the next inning he started another three-run outburst with a long home run into the right-field stands. The Cards had a 6-0 lead. The Yanks cut this lead in half when Mantle belted a three-run homer in the sixth, but Gibson and his teammates hung on, winning the game and the Series, 7-5.

It had been an amazing season for Lou Brock. He had started the season as just another player for the Cubs and had finished it as a .300-hitting star for the Cardinals. In the Series he proved it was no fluke, batting an even .300 with 9 hits in 30 trips. He also had 5 RBI's in 7 games. In one year, Lou was on top of the baseball world.

Brock was now confident of his job and himself. The sweet smell of success had touched him and stayed with him. He wanted to stay on top, and that meant working even harder to harness his natural talents. He started work right away in the spring. Even the exhibition games were important to him now, because he was always watching, studying every move every pitcher made.

When he got on base—even in an exhibition game—he began testing, experimenting, and learning just how far he could get off the bag and how to pick just the right moment to make his move. At the plate he concentrated on hitting the ball to all fields—making contact, bunting, and doing everything that would make him more of a threat. When he was working out on his own, he practiced his starts, his acceleration, his sprinting, and his sliding. He remembered how little he'd improved during his years with the Cubs. He didn't want that to happen again.

And it didn't. During the next two seasons Lou firmly established himself as a consistent star and a dependable player who made things happen. His batting averages in 1965 and 1966 were .288 and .285. He had 16 homers and 69 RBI's one year, 15 homers and 46 RBI's the next. His stolen base totals were 63 and 74, beginning his string of 50 or more steals per year, as he quickly perfected his running techniques.

If Brock had any weakness it was in the field, where he was still sometimes prone to error. But with his speed, he also caught up with balls that other outfielders couldn't reach. Because of his aggressive play he sometimes gambled in the outfield. This led to miscues but also to potential great plays, and since he didn't make as many errors as in his Cub days, no one really complained.

At the plate Lou was becoming a complete hitter. Unlike many other base stealers, who tend to be strictly singles hitters, Lou was a threat to hit the long ball. He saw this clearly as an advantage.

"A pitcher will challenge a good base runner more often because he wants to keep him off the basepaths," said Lou. "But because they know I can hit it out, I'm not challenged quite as often."

Pitcher Claude Osteen, a crafty left-hander then with the Dodgers, concurred about Lou's skills at bat:

"Lou has no specific weaknesses up there, and you just have to mix up your pitches and hope for the best. If he gets on, he has so many different moves and so much speed, it's almost impossible to contain him."

The respect for Brock was growing every year. However, the Cards slipped back in 1965 and 1966 (yielding the N.L. crown to the Dodgers), but after the 1966 season, Dodger pitching ace Sandy Koufax retired and the pennant was up for grabs once more. And the Cards were one of the top contending teams.

And as usual, with the pressure on and a good pennant race in the works, Lou Brock was at his best. He hit .299 in 1967, garnering 206 hits in 689 at bats. He was in the lineup day in and day out. He also had his best power year, slamming out 21 homers and driving home 76 runs. He scored 113 times and swiped another 52 bases. With a performance like that, it wasn't surprising that he helped the Cardinals to another National League pennant. This time St. Louis would be facing the Boston Red Sox in the World Series.

Before the series started, one Red Sox scout gave his evaluation of the opposition:

"The key to the series for us is stopping Brock. He's the hub of their attack, the one who gets it all going. If he gets a single, it's as good as a double, and no one likes to see a man on second right off the bat. If we can keep Brock off the bases, we've got a great shot at winning."

There was one big question mark for the Cards. Their pitching ace, Bob Gibson, had been out of action with a broken leg from June 15 to September 7. Gibson had worked himself back into shape, but there was still a question of whether he could take the grind of perhaps three series starts. But Gibson was on the mound for game one, facing Boston's Jose Santiago. Red Sox ace Jim Lonborg, a 22-game winner, needed another day of rest after pitching the pennant-clincher on the last day of the season; he would be held for game two.

Gibson and Santiago matched serves for two innings. Then in the third, a familiar pattern emerged. Lou Brock hit a single. Then Curt Flood doubled, Brock taking third. Brock then sped home as Roger Maris grounded out. Pitcher Santiago surprised everyone by clouting a homer in the bottom of the inning to tie it. It stayed that way until the seventh when Brock came up once more.

Once again Brock slapped a base hit to the outfield. He danced off first, watching Santiago. Then he was off. Catcher Russ Gibson fired to second, but it was too late. Brock had his first series steal. A minute later it was evident just what a potent weapon the steal was. Brock breezed to third on an infield out and then scored on another infield out. Without the steal the run wouldn't have come home. The Cards took the game, 2-1, with Brock scoring both runs.

The second game was a different story. The Red Sox applied rule number one: they stopped Brock. In fact, Jim Lonborg stopped nearly everyone, pitching a brilliant one-hitter as the Sox won, 5-0, and evened the series. The series now moved to St. Louis, where the fans hoped their heroes would get rolling again.

First inning, Brock was up. Itchy from his hitless second game, Lou swung from the heels and drove a triple to right center. Flood followed with a single, and the Cards were on the board. A two-run homer by Mike Shannon made it 3-0 in the second. The Sox got one off Nelson Briles in the sixth, but then Brock went to work again.

This time Brock showed his speed by beating out a bunt. He danced off first, and when a pickoff throw went wild, he raced all the way to third. He then scored on a single by Maris. Each club got one more run, and the game ended up a 5-2 Cardinal win.

The fourth game was over before it began. Brock

started it with another single; this was followed by a Flood base hit. Maris doubled both men home, and before the inning ended, the Redbirds had four runs. They got two more later, and Bob Gibson breezed past the Sox with a five-hit shutout. It was now 3-1, and the Series seemed to be in the bag.

In the next game Lonborg took the mound, and once again he applied his formula for success. Pitching brilliantly for a second time, the big right-hander stifled Brock and the Cards by pitching a three-hitter and winning a 3-1 victory.

Back in Fenway Park, the Sox had new life. They gambled with a young pitcher, Gary Waslewski, who held the Birds long enough for the Sox bats to go to work. Boston won it, 8-4, to tie the Series at three-games each. Brock had two hits and another steal, but this time his club lost. Now it was down to the final game. The Cards had Gibson, ready after three days' rest, while Boston would have to gamble with Lonborg, who had been brilliant but would be pitching with just two days' rest.

The game was scoreless for two innings, as the capacity crowd at ancient Fenway screamed on every pitch. But knowledgeable people in the press box didn't think it would last long.

"Lonborg's laboring," one writer said. "He's not throwing with the same smooth motion he had, and his fastball doesn't have the good hop."

Most of the others nodded in agreement. They also agreed that Gibson looked as sharp as ever and was flipping the ball up with a loose, effortless motion. Gibby was one of baseball's great competitors. If a team was going to get him, they usually had to do it early. Given a lead in the late innings, he usually got tougher and tougher, like most of the great ones. And the fire in Gibson's eyes was burning after just two.

In the third inning Lonborg's magic spell came to an end. A triple by weak-hitting Dal Maxvill started it. Singles by Flood and Maris and a wild pitch accounted for the first two runs. Then in the fifth the Redbirds struck again. First, pitcher Gibson aided his own cause with a home run. Then Brock rapped another single. Sensing the kill, he promptly stole second and then third. The unnerved Lonborg gave up a sacrifice fly to Maris, and it was 4-0.

Three more runs in the sixth settled the issue. Gibson weakened momentarily in the fifth and eighth, giving up a single tallies; but he pitched out of trouble to notch his third series win, 7-2, and to give the world's championship to the Cards.

His great pitching earned Gibson the MVP title for the Series, but Lou Brock was right behind. Brock had a tremendous series, collecting 12 hits in 29 at bats for a .414 average. He also swiped 7 bases, erasing any doubts that he was now the premier base stealer in the majors.

The Cards continued to roll in 1968. Lou's stats fell off slightly, to a .279 average with just 6 homers and 51 RBI's; but he swiped 62 bases and was still the catalyst in many Redbird rallies, as the Cards took another N.L. title. So it was back to the Series, this time against the Detroit Tigers and their 31-game winner, Denny McLain.

But the Cards had Gibson again. Healthy all year, he had turned in a super season, winning 22 games, losing 9, and compiling a record-breaking 1.12 earned run average. When Gibson shut out the Tigers and whipped McLain, 4-0, in the opener, the pattern seemed to be established.

Still, it was the World Series, and the fall classic often produces unlikely heroes. In game two, the Tigers number-two pitcher, Mickey Lolich, handcuffed the

Cards, 8-1, to even it up. The Cards took the third game, 7-3, as Brock starred with 3 hits and 3 stolen bases. Gibson then whipped McLain again, pitching brilliantly in a 10-1 Cardinal win. It was now 3 games to 1, and looked locked in. Brock had three more hits in that game, including a homer, a steal, and four RBI's. He was playing more brilliantly than ever.

Lolich came back to whip the Cards, 5-3, in game five, despite three more Brock hits, including a pair of doubles. The Tigers still had life though, and they finally got a strong game from McLain, who won game six easily, 13-1, as the Tigers produced a ten-run third inning. Brock had just one hit in this one.

So it came down to a seventh game once again. Both teams had their best pitchers ready. It was Gibson against Lolich. The Cards were favored.

For six innings the game was a classic pitching duel. Neither pitcher budged. Then, in the top of the seventh, the Tigers came to life. With two out Norm Cash and Willie Horton each singled. Then Jim Northrup slammed a drive to center. Curt Flood, one of the best outfielders in the business, lost the ball among the white shirts of the huge crowd, giving Northrup a two-run triple. Bill Freehan then singled, and the Tigers had a three-run lead.

Lolich made it stand up. Both clubs scored in the ninth, but the Tigers won it, 4-1, coming back from a 3-1 Series deficit to take all the marbles. Lolich's third victory gave him the MVP award. Lou Brock again finished second. Lou had had another great Series, with 13 hits in 28 at bats for a .464 average. And once again he had stolen 7 bases, walloped 2 homers, and driven in 5 runs. But his performance didn't matter to him. His team had lost. And as with all the great ones, winning always comes first with Brock.

To everyone else, Brock was always a big winner.

Though the Cards faltered during the next several seasons, Brock seemed to improve with age. From 1969 to 1973, Brock's batting averages were .298, .304, .313, .311, and .297. Each year he came to bat well over 600 times, and he had between 193 and 202 hits in each of those seasons. And of course, he was over the 50-steal mark each time.

Respect for Brock continued to grow in all corners of the baseball world. Hall of Famer Ted Williams, not a man usually given to compliments, said:

"Lou Brock is one hell of a base stealer. And he's even more effective because he gets the pitcher and catcher and the rest of the infield all on edge worrying about his stealing a base."

"He's the only base stealer who can actually outrun the little white ball," said Mets pitcher Jerry Koosman.

"How do you deal with the guy?" asked Bob Skinner, a former teammate of Brock's. "You can't walk him, because when you do, it's like giving him a double. Whatever you try, he always seems to be creating winning situations, whether by hitting the long ball or bunting, or getting on base by making the other team hurry the play."

A former major league first baseman, frustrated by years of trying to hold Brock close and then watching him steal second, still found it hard to work up any animosity toward him:

"Lou never seems as intense as, say, Maury Wills. Maury would get on first and never say a word. You were the enemy, and he was concentrating on getting to second. Lou is different. He'll smile and say hello, maybe ask you about yourself or your family. But as soon as he's ready . . . bam . . . he's gone."

Brock's own manager at the time, Red Schoendeinst, summed it up easily: "Lou Brock is just the most exciting player in baseball!"

It was Brock's outwardly cheerful nature and quick smile that led a writer to call him "the congenial superstar," a distinction he earned by his cooperative nature with the press and fans. But Brock's smile was something of a mask, too, as he would readily admit.

"People see me smiling when I'm on the field," he said. "But they don't always understand it. They don't know I smile the broadest when I'm the angriest."

Brock also has some definite ideas about sport and the athlete's responsibility to the public and to himself.

"Sport is current," he says. "People don't really come out to cheer for a Bob Gibson, a Lou Brock. They come out to cheer for the sport. People have been cheering these sports for years and years. My role is to play; their role is to cheer. The day after I retire there'll be someone else sliding into second base. And they'll be cheering just as hard."

In a sense, Brock has never received the widespread recognition that other stars, even some lesser ones, have gotten. This bothers him, though he's been mollified somewhat in recent years by a salary well over the $100,000 mark. He also knows that his peers—his teammates and others—are well aware of his presence on the field:

"When the chips are down, the ballplayers know what I can do to make this club a winner."

Brock's years in the game have helped him formulate a life style, a kind of philosophy that governs his actions. And as the years passed, the private Brock slowly became known to the public audience.

"Money per se doesn't turn me on anymore," he said a few years ago. "A lot of athletes are on ego-trips, *thing* trips. When I see a rookie making $14,000 wearing a $200 suit, and driving an $8,000 car, I ask him: 'Why do you want to pretend you're something you're not?' He tells me: 'The public wants me to live up to a certain image, I gotta look like a pro.' I tell him: 'Baby, you're a fool. You should be wearing *jeans.*' "

In a sense, Brock has come full circle from his poverty-stricken childhood:

"My dreams don't center around getting more money. The more money I get, the more I want to get back to what I had to give up to make it: the simple life, the normal life.

"And the other side of the ego trip—fame—that doesn't turn me on, either. I've got a friend, a great ballplayer who's washed up. He should quit, but he can't. It's not the money—he has plenty already. It's the women, the road trips, the clubhouse, the fans, the spotlight. Baseball isn't just his livelihood anymore; it's his *life*.

"Well, the day I lose the touch, believe me, I'll quit. I'll retire. Retire, retire!"

Brock may not be obsessed by money, but he knows that life is infinitely easier when money isn't a constant worry. So he wants to be comfortable without having his life controlled by money and the desire or need to make more. He has solved this problem by making sound and long-lasting investments. He explains:

"Investing is a hobby with me, and that way I can enjoy it. I try to keep my investments diversified. I screen offers, I seek out things and decide whether it makes sound economic sense for me to get involved in them. During the offseason I travel a lot, do things like going to meetings, seminars, and investigating the politics involved in each venture. I get just as much satisfaction out of investing as I do out of baseball."

It all started with a flower shop, in which Lou posed on television for a Yellow Pages commercial. But since then he has become involved in, as he says, "more sophisticated" things. Brock isn't making the mistake of so many athletes. He's preparing for his future now, while he's still on top. So many stars wait until retirement to plan, only to find that their names no longer have the magic they did when they were in their athletic prime.

But at the same time, Lou Brock hasn't lost sight of his origins. He has always been interested in helping youngsters. Around 1965 he was the guest speaker at the Tandy Boys Club in St. Louis. After he finished speaking, someone told him the club was almost bankrupt. Lou didn't want to see all those kids lose a good thing, so he went on a speaking tour of his own just to raise some money for the club. And he didn't stop there. He took such a continuing active interest in the club that before long it was renamed the "Lou Brock Boys Club."

"Lou's the kind of guy who doesn't showcase the things he does for others," said Bill Alphin, who was a club director. "Let me give you an example. One day a box of trophies just turned up, enough trophies to last us at least five years. There was a little note in the box. 'From a friend,' it read. We just smiled and shook our heads. You know, as if to say, 'Well, Lou did it again.'"

Bill Alphin went on to say that it wasn't so much a matter of money, it was also the time Lou gave to the club. "It's just unbelievable when Lou comes in there. The kids just go wild."

As usual, Brock has given a great deal of thought to his role at the Club and in helping youngsters.

"There are a number of reasons why I'm dedicated

to the Boys Club," he said. "One is the memory of my own childhood. Like so many other kids, I was basically uninformed. I could have gone in either direction, good or bad. People sometimes forget that baseball is a game of decisions. The kid has to learn how to make decisions. Sport teaches him to be decisive, and I think it can carry over into life.

"I also believe an athlete can get a kid's attention when a non-athlete can't. I remember when I was a kid, people were always telling me a lot of different things, warning me against this, suggesting that. But very little of that advice really registered because I was usually not paying attention.

"It was that way when I first started playing baseball. My high school coach was always lecturing me about hitting, running, throwing, all that stuff. But I never really gave a second thought to the things he was saying. Then one day Hank Aaron came in to run a baseball clinic. He was the first pro athlete I'd ever seen. He started saying all the same things my coach had been saying for years, and all of a sudden they made sense. So it was because a pro said them that I suddenly became highly motivated. And that's the way it is with a lot of kids. This is the kind of thing that triggered my involvement with kids. I started out with the idea of giving them someone to identify with the way I identified with Aaron."

Lou also realizes that good advice is essential to the mature man, and he knows that many of his fellow pros have been victims of bad or wrong advice.

"Most athletes need advice when they turn pro," says Brock. "So the question becomes where do they get it? Usually the hangups begin when they go to their friends, because friends aren't qualified to give the athlete the kind of help he needs. Some go to agents, who can acquire money for them but have no special expertise on how to retain that money. That's the problem with the athlete—not how to get money, but how to hold onto it.

"And that makes good advice all the more essential for the black athlete. He must realize there isn't going to be a job waiting for him at the end of his career. So he can't allow himself to think in terms of 'job.' He has to create his own job, make himself independent."

Lou Brock has done this with his investments and business interests. He has created, through hard work and intelligence, a place for himself in the world once his playing days are ended.

But as of early 1974, there was no indication that his playing days were nearing any kind of end. In fact, he was off and running right from the start, and his stolen-base pace was so high that people were already looking twice. Brock had had a few self-doubts at the beginning of the 1973 season. But after receiving a vote of confidence and encouragement from Maury Wills, he began running the bases like a twenty-one-year-old. And at age thirty-five, he was still finding new ways to turn situations to his own advantage.

One catcher who gave Brock trouble for years was Jerry Grote, who for years was the Mets' backstop. As Brock has said, Grote is "quick out of the box, has a powerful arm, and always seemed to have a sixth sense about my stealing." So, for a time, Brock rarely tried to steal when Grote was catching. Then, one day in early 1974, things changed.

"Grote walked past me before a game, and I said hello to him," Lou recalls. "He either didn't hear me or was ignoring me so I said hello a second time. Again he didn't answer. So I screamed at him, 'Hello Grote!' That seemed to bother him, and he was still upset about it when I came to bat. So when I got on I began screaming again. 'Grote! Grote! Grote!' He wanted me to go, of course. So I went. And I finally beat him. Since that day I've run at about a ninety-percent efficiency against him."

Brock has always maintained, however, that he runs to win ballgames, not for records, and that claim would be difficult to dispute. But like most top base runners, Lou has a special kind of antipathy toward first base.

"First base is nowhere," he says, "and most times it's useless to stay there. On the other hand, second base is probably the safest place on the field. When I steal second, I practically eliminate the double play, and I can score on almost anything hit past the infield."

Brock continued to prove his point by stealing second at every opportunity. By the time the team had played 56 games, roughly one-third of the schedule, he had stolen 40 bases. People were beginning to talk about his making a run at Wills' record. As usual, he was hitting above the .300 mark, which put him on base often enough to have a shot. (A .250 or even a .280 hitter simply isn't on first base often enough to break the stolen base mark.)

By the time the team had played half its games, Brock had 50 steals. By August 1, he had 66, though some thought his pace was slowing, that his age was finally beginning to take its toll. But in a weekend series against the Phils, he swiped 8 bases in 9 attempts, giving him 74 steals in 109 games, and talk of a record began anew. A further advantage was that the Cardinals were in a pennant race for the first time in years, and everybody knew that Lou Brock always played his best when the chips were down.

When Brock got steal number 90 in the team's hundred and thirtieth game, it became obvious that only an injury or other form of catastrophe could prevent him from smashing the mark. The publicity came in increasing waves, and more people than ever were becoming aware of Lou's great talents.

Then, in September, came some added, unexpected pressure. Both Brock and Cardinal rookie center-fielder Bake McBride, received a letter threatening their lives. The letter was filled with racial slurs and written by a man who claimed he was terminally ill and had nothing to live for. He said he was going to shoot both Brock and McBride right at the ball park.

Star ballplayers sometimes receive crank letters but this one had more of a true ring to it, and both out-fielders were put under twenty-four-hour guard.

"I can't say this doesn't bother me," admitted Lou. "Whenever someone threatens to kill you it's real; the fear is there. Both Bake and I have got to try to forget about it."

Fortunately, the threat was never anything more than that, and Brock continued to run. He got steal number 100 against the Mets on September 6; he then tied and broke the record in the same game, against the Phils, on September 10.

"I never thought it would happen," admitted Lou, "but now that it did I'm glad it's over. I can't really say I care about records because I'm not on an ego trip. I just steal to win. But maybe when I'm seventy-five I'll care."

The old record holder, Wills, admitted *he* cared, and had mixed emotions when Brock set the new standard.

"I always felt it was my record," said Wills, "and I didn't think anyone would approach it so soon, not even in my lifetime. I don't think anyone looks forward to seeing his own record broken. So, honestly, I was hoping he wouldn't do it, but once he got around eighty it became very obvious. And don't get me wrong. I never wished Lou any tough luck. My hat's off to him."

More recognition soon came. The late Casey Stengel called Brock one of the four best base runners he'd ever seen, citing Ty Cobb, Max Carey, and Wills as the other three. And by the time Brock finished (with 118 steals, a .306 batting average, 194 hits, and 104 runs scored), his brilliance was being written about all over the country.

"The shame of it is," wrote one scribe, "that the Cards didn't win the pennant. Because then the entire country would have had the pleasure of seeing Lou Brock perform in another World Series, where his sheer artistry becomes more evident than ever."

But Brock didn't get full recognition. Steve Garvey of the Dodgers, who also had an outstanding year, won the National League's Most Valuable Player award, with Lou a close second. It bothered Lou, though he admitted that Garvey had had an MVP-type season, and since the Dodgers had won the National League pennant, the odds had been tipped in Garvey's favor.

Many people felt Lou deserved it. Limited to just 136 games in 1975 because of some minor injuries, Lou nevertheless hit .309 and swiped 56 more bases, giving him a lifetime total of 809 steals and putting him well within striking range of Ty Cobb's all-time mark of 892.

In many ways, 1975 was another remarkable year for the 36-year-old Brock. He had his fifth .300 year in the last six (he hit .297 the year he missed), and still managed 56 steals at an age where many athletes were already retired. He was also highly honored at the outset of the year when he received the Roberto Clemente Award, given annually to the player who best exemplifies the ideals of baseball, both on and off the field.

During the off-season Lou underwent surgery on his left hand for the repair of some tendon damage, but he was fully recovered and ready for action again in 1976. And now people began asking him about Cobb's lifetime mark.

"I'm sure I can't do it this year," Lou said. "That would be asking a little too much. But if I stay healthy and things go as they should, I think I can break the record next season."

That was the way most people felt. Lou needed 84 more steals to do it. Some were skeptical, figuring at his age he could suddenly lose it. In other words, they doubted that 84 more steals could be pulled from the now nearly 37-year-old body.

The Cards decided to spot Lou more in 1976; in other words, to rest him in second games of double-headers and in some day games following night games, a practice sometimes used with aging stars, although they trusted Lou's judgment and pretty much let him call the shots.

To the surprise of perhaps a few, Lou continued to be a very productive ballplayer in 1976. Unfortunately, the team was in a period of transition, with many young ballplayers coming in, and they slipped below the .500 mark and stayed there. Had there been a hot pennant race, Brock undoubtedly would have played more. Everyone knows what kind of a ball-player he is when the chips are down.

At any rate, Lou appeared in 133 games in 1976 and once again hit above .300, finishing at .301. He had 150 hits, hit four home runs, and amazingly had his best RBI season in 10 years with 67. And perhaps even more amazingly, the slender outfielder stole another 56 bases, giving him 865 for his career and extending his 50 or better consecutive steal mark to an even dozen years.

So Lou entered the 1977 season with some impressive numbers. First there were the 865 steals. Right behind that was his total of 2,701 hits, third among active players behind Brooks Robinson (since retired) and Pete Rose. So there was already some murmuring about Lou getting 3,000 career hits, and only a select handful of players have ever done that. Plus his lifetime batting average stood at a solid .296.

The excitement about the stolen base record began building at the outset of the season. In St. Louis there was a big countdown board in the outfield showing how many steals Lou needed to surpass Cobb. And the so-called experts were projecting that Lou would break the mark in late July or early August. All this combined to put added pressure on the slender shoulders of Lou Brock.

"There was far more pressure on Lou to surpass Cobb's lifetime mark than there was for the season mark," relates Card GM Bing Devine. "He surpassed the season record and went on from there. But the Cobb record . . . well, he had grown three years older in the meantime. He recognized that something could happen to him at any age. Let's face it, if he broke an ankle or damaged a knee at age 38 he might not be able to come back to perform well. Period. Particularly as far as stealing is concerned.

"So I think the pressure grew on him over a period of years and in '77 reached a point where it really had an impact on his ability to perform up to his norm, especially during the middle months of the year."

Lou didn't get off to a fast start. But that had happened before, notably in 1973, and he wasn't worried. His batting average was well below .300 and the stolen bases weren't coming. He was being thrown out as often as he was making it, and he wasn't trying to steal all that much. It didn't take long before he was hearing how he was behind the projection and had to steal so many bases to catch up. And then there were some skeptics who figured he wouldn't make it at all in '77.

"He admitted he was under tremendous pressure," says Bing Devine. "Don't forget, to steal a base you've got to get on base, and then you've got to concern yourself with the condition of the game and the score, and the state of the club, and the race, and so forth. It did affect him. He became quite nervous, quite frustrated, really unsettled, more than I've ever seen him."

Many of the young Cardinals, players like shortstop Garry Templeton, first baseman Keith Hernandez, and outfielder Tony Scott, were coming into their own, and combined with veterans Ted Simmons, Ken Reitz, Brock, and others, actually had the Cardinals in the pennant race until well after mid-season, when the Philadelphia Phillies got hot and blew everyone out.

But the games were all meaningful in the early going, and as Bing Devine said, Lou had to be concerned with a number of things, not just stealing a base.

July came and went, the season moved into August, and Lou was finally getting there, but ever so slowly. He barely had 20 steals, and it was obvious that his mark of 12 straight 50-steal seasons would be coming to an end. But there was still the record. His average had crept up to the .260s, but that's a far cry from .300 and means that many fewer hits, fewer times on base, and fewer chances to steal.

"There was also a lot of attention in every city he went into during the year," recalls Bing Devine. "Everyone knew what a great accomplishment he was nearing and the fans were stimulated to come see him play, especially when he started getting close. Everywhere we went they were getting up press conferences for him, spcial lunches, special awards, and I know all of this wore on him.

"As for his decreased playing time, I think he recognized this as a necessity. As the year wore on he realized it was a desirable schedule for him and he'll probably have to follow that type of schedule even more as time progresses."

Finally, in mid-August he was getting close. "I'd like to break the record in front of the fans in St. Louis," Lou said. "They've been very loyal and supportive during my whole career."

But Lou wasn't one to let opportunity slip away. The team was in San Diego on August 29, and Lou had 891 steals. In the first inning he singled. Then he took off for second.

Breaking quickly, using his long strides, and still using the straight-in, pop-up slide as he had for so long, he hit second in a cloud of dust. The umpire signaled safe! It was his 27th steal of the year and the 892nd of his career. He had tied the mark.

He didn't waste much time breaking it. That came in the seventh inning of the same game. Once again he swiped second, made it look easy, and had a record to cherish forever.

The game was stopped and Lou was given second base as a memento. With typical Brock graciousness, he said, "I'm glad it's over and that I've broken the record. But I also think we should always remember the ballplayer whose record I broke, Ty Cobb."

As for Bing Devine, he saw the change in Lou once the record had fallen.

"The night he broke the record you could almost see the load lifted from his shoulders. He played more relaxed and more normally the final month of the season."

Unfortunately, the Phillies had already run away from the rest of the National League East, so Lou didn't have a pennant race to think about. Still, at age 38, he had what must be considered a fine season, especially with the pressure of the record.

In 141 games he batted .272 with 133 hits and 46 runs batted in. He finished the season with 35 steals, giving him an even 900 for his career. However, the 35 steals were accompanied by 24 throw-outs, far higher than his usual average, and that was part of the pressure and perhaps part of his advancing age.

Lou's 133 hits also raised his career total to 2,834, making 3,000 a very realistic goal. But now, perhaps, it will be a battle against time as much as anything else.

"As with the stolen base record, Lou doesn't talk openly about getting 3,000 hits," said Bing Devine. "I get the feeling he doesn't particularly like to talk about it. But I was with him at a dinner recently when someone asked him outright whether he set a goal of 3,000 hits, and he confirmed it. But I think it's recognized by everybody concerned that at his age and on a limited play basis, it's hardly likely he'll do it in one year. It will probably take two."

Asked if it will be the same kind of pressure situation as the stolen base mark, Devine answered this way:

"I saw Musial go through the same thing, and he was a great pressure guy. I don't say it had any violent effect on his ability or his contribution during that period, but getting to 3,000 hits weighed on him. It was a relief when he achieved it. Maybe because Lou has accomplished his one main goal it will take away the pressure, but it seems that any player shooting for a milestone and getting to what's considered an advanced age for an athlete, recognizes that something may happen that will forestall his ability to do it."

So Lou will return to the Cards and undoubtedly play as long as he feels he can contribute. He's always taken care of his body, and it has yet to betray him. The feeling seems to be that the Cards are a pitcher or two away from real contention, and nothing would make Lou Brock young again faster than a tight pennant race.

In the meantime, he continues to be one of the most popular Cardinals and most popular athletes in St. Louis. In fact, back in 1975 the fans voted him the "Most Memorable Personality" in Cardinal history and voted his 105th stolen base as the "Most Memorable Moment." Of course these are today's fans who don't remember the colorful Cards of the past, but it nevertheless shows the tremendous respect and popularity held by Lou Brock.

He's earned it in many ways. Bing Devine also talked about the contributions Lou has made to his community during the years.

"Lou's always done a lot of charitable work with kids," Devine said. "At one time he had a great deal to do with the formation of and the advancement of the Boys' Club here, the Boys' Club of St. Louis, I think it was called. In fact, the headquarters and facilities for that club are on the site of the old Sportsman's Park in north St. Louis where the Cards used to play.

"Then just the other day [November of 1977] Lou was made Honorary Chairman of the Multiple Sclerosis drive in Missouri for next year. And he's done a lot of things and made a lot of appearances in connection with young people here that haven't really gotten much attention.

"Maybe the best way to put it into perspective is to say that also in November Lou was given the St. Louis Award, which is considered a rather special thing here. It's an award for distinguished service to the community and has always gone to industrialists, philanthropists, and other prominent people. Lou is the first athlete to receive it. That's how the people here feel about him.

"The Cardinals have had a lot of colorful personalities down through the years," Devine continued, "and a good number of them are in the Hall of Fame—players like Sisler, Hornsby, Pepper Martin, Joe Medwick, Frankie Frisch, Dizzy Dean, and up to Musial. Lou just follows in the footsteps of some greats, whose shoes he fills very well, and I'm almost certain in my mind that five years after he retires he'll be voted alongside them in the Hall of Fame."

That's quite a tribute to a very great ballplayer, one who has proved himself through his deeds and through his consistency for many years.

Who would have thought it of the young, raw, unrefined kid who came up with the Cubs in 1962? For a while it looked as if his speed and talent would never be channeled in the right direction. But, as always, Brock accepted the challenge and became one of the most exciting and respected players of his generation. Perhaps it was the Mets' Bud Harrelson who best summed up the feeling toward Lou Brock around the entire league:

"I'm happy for Lou," said Harrelson. "He has done a lot for base stealers, and I root for him. He's a good friend of mine. He's good for baseball. He's never shamed the game."

Lou Brock, King of the Baserunners, is truly a popular champion.

★ STATISTICS ★

Rod Carew

Year	Club	G	AB	R	H	2B	3B	HR	RBI	SB	BA
1964	Melb.	37	123	17	40	5	3	0	21	14	.325
1965	Orlando	125	439	57	133	20	8	1	52	52	.303
1966	Wilson	112	383	64	112	19	3	1	30	28	.292
1967	Minn.	137	514	66	150	22	7	8	51	5	.292
1968	Minn.	127	461	46	126	27	2	1	42	12	.273
1969	Minn.	123	458	79	152	30	4	8	56	19	.332
1970	Minn.	51	191	27	70	12	3	4	28	4	.366
1971	Minn.	147	577	88	177	16	10	2	48	6	.307
1972	Minn.	142	535	61	170	21	6	0	51	12	.318
1973	Minn.	149	580	98	203	30	11	6	62	41	.350
1974	Minn.	153	599	86	218	30	5	3	55	38	.364
1975	Minn.	143	535	89	192	24	4	14	80	35	.359
1976	Minn.	156	605	97	200	29	12	9	90	49	.331
1977	Minn.	155	616	128	239	38	16	14	100	23	.388
Maj. L. Totals		1483	5671	865	1897	279	80	69	663	244	.334

Steve Garvey

Year	Club	G	AB	R	H	2B	3B	HR	RBI	BA
1968	Ogden	62	216	49	73	12	3	20	59	.338
1969	Albuq.	83	316	51	118	18	2	14	85	.373
	L.A.	3	3	0	1	0	0	0	0	.333
1970	L.A.	34	93	8	25	5	0	1	6	.269
	Spokane	95	376	71	120	26	5	15	87	.319
1971	L.A.	81	225	27	51	12	1	7	26	.227
1972	L.A.	96	294	36	79	14	2	9	30	.269
1973	L.A.	114	349	37	106	17	3	8	50	.304
1974	L.A.	156	642	95	200	32	3	21	111	.312
1975	L.A.	160	659	85	210	38	6	18	95	.319
1976	L.A.	162	631	85	200	37	4	13	80	.317
1977	L.A.	162	646	91	192	25	3	33	115	.297
Maj. L. Totals		968	3542	464	1064	180	22	110	513	.300

Thurman Munson

Year	Club	G	AB	R	H	2B	3B	HR	RBI	BA
1968	Bingham.	71	226	28	68	12	3	6	37	.301
1969	Syracuse	28	102	13	37	9	1	2	17	.363
	N.Y.	26	86	6	22	1	2	1	9	.256
1970	N.Y.	132	423	59	137	25	4	6	53	.302
1971	N.Y.	125	451	71	113	15	4	10	42	.251
1972	N.Y.	140	511	54	143	16	3	7	46	.280
1973	N.Y.	147	519	80	156	29	4	20	74	.301
1974	N.Y.	144	517	64	135	19	2	13	60	.261
1975	N.Y.	157	597	83	190	24	3	12	102	.318
1976	N.Y.	152	616	79	186	27	1	17	105	.302
1977	N.Y.	149	595	85	183	28	5	18	100	.308
Maj. L. Totals		1172	4345	581	1265	184	28	104	591	.291

Lou Brock

Year	Club	G	AB	R	H	2B	3B	HR	RBI	SB	BA
1961	St. Cld.	128	501	117	181	33	6	14	82	38	.361
	Chicago	4	11	1	1	0	0	0	0	0	.091
1962	Chicago	123	434	73	114	24	7	9	35	16	.263
1963	Chicago	148	547	79	141	19	11	9	37	24	.258
1964	Chicago	52	215	30	54	9	2	2	14	10	.251
	St. L.	103	419	81	146	21	9	12	44	33	.348
1965	St. L.	155	631	107	182	35	8	16	69	63	.288
1966	St. L.	156	643	94	183	24	12	15	46	74	.285
1967	St. L.	159	689	113	206	32	12	21	76	52	.299
1968	St. L.	159	660	92	184	46	14	6	51	62	.279
1969	St. L.	157	655	97	195	33	10	12	47	53	.298
1970	St. L.	155	664	114	202	29	5	13	57	51	.304
1971	St. L.	157	640	126	200	37	7	7	61	64	.313
1972	St. L.	153	621	81	193	26	8	3	42	63	.311
1973	St. L.	160	650	110	193	29	8	7	63	70	.297
1974	St. L.	153	635	105	194	25	7	3	48	118	.306
1975	St. L.	136	528	78	163	27	6	3	47	56	.309
1976	St. L.	133	498	73	150	24	5	4	67	56	.301
1977	St. L.	141	489	69	133	22	6	2	46	35	.272
Maj. L. Totals		2404	9629	1523	2834	462	137	144	850	900	.294